In Sea
Produ

MW01223232

A Guide To
Resource Allocation
In Education

Lawrence O. Picus

ERIC Clearinghouse on Educational Management
College of Education
University of Oregon
2001

In Search of More Productive Schools: A Guide to Resource Allocation in Education

Editorial Director: Stuart C. Smith

Design: Leeann August

Library of Congress Cataloging-in-Publication Data

Picus, Larry, 1954-
   In search of more productive schools: a guide to resource allocation in education /
Lawrence O. Picus.—1st ed.
      p. cm.
   Includes bibliographical references (p.).
   ISBN 0-86552-147-6
      1. Education—United States—Finance. 2. Public schools —United States—Cost
effectiveness. 3. Resource allocation. I. Title.

LB2825 .P475 2001
379.1'3'0973—dc21

00-050378

Type: 12/14.4 AGaramond

Printer: McNaughton & Gunn, Inc., Saline, Michigan

THE ASSOCIATION
OF EDUCATIONAL
PUBLISHERS

Ed Press

FIRST EDITION
Printed in the United States of America, 2001

ERIC Clearinghouse on Educational Management
   5207 University of Oregon
   Eugene, OR 97403-5207
   Telephone: (541) 346-5044 Fax: (541) 346-2334
   World Wide Web: http://eric.uoregon.edu
ERIC/CEM Accession Number: EA 030 613

This publication was prepared in part with funding from the Office of Educational
Research and Improvement, U.S. Department of Education, under contract no. OERI-
RR 93002006. The opinions expressed in this report do not necessarily reflect the
positions or policies of the Department of Education. No federal funds were used in
the printing of this publication.

The University of Oregon is an equal opportunity, affirmative action institution
committed to cultural diversity.

MISSION OF ERIC AND THE CLEARINGHOUSE

The Educational Resources Information Center (ERIC) is a national information system operated by the U.S. Department of Education. ERIC serves the educational community by disseminating research results and other resource information that can be used in developing more effective educational programs.

The ERIC Clearinghouse on Educational Management, one of several such units in the system, was established at the University of Oregon in 1966. The Clearinghouse and its companion units process research reports and journal articles for announcement in ERIC's index and abstract bulletins.

Research reports are announced in Resources in Education (RIE), available in many libraries and by subscription from the United States Government Printing Office, Washington, D.C. 20402-9371.

Most of the documents listed in RIE can be purchased through the ERIC Document Reproduction Service, operated by Cincinnati Bell Information Systems.

Journal articles are announced in Current Index to Journals in Education. CIJE is also available in many libraries and can be ordered from Oryx Press, 4041 North Central Avenue at Indian School, Suite 700, Phoenix, Arizona 85012. Semiannual cumulations can be ordered separately.

Besides processing documents and journal articles, the Clearinghouse prepares bibliographies, literature reviews, monographs, and other interpretive research studies on topics in its educational area.

CLEARINGHOUSE NATIONAL ADVISORY BOARD

George Babigian, Executive Director, American Education Finance Association
Anne L. Bryant, Executive Director, National School Boards Association
Vincent L. Ferrandino, National Association of Elementary School Principals
Paul Houston, Executive Director, American Association of School
    Administrators
Karen Seashore Louis, Vice President, Division A, American Educational Research
    Association
John T. MacDonald, Director, State Leadership Center, Council of Chief State
    School Officers
Gerald Tirozzi, Executive Director, National Association of Secondary School
    Principals
Michelle Young, Executive Director, University Council for Educational
    Administration

ADMINISTRATIVE STAFF

Philip K. Piele, Professor and Director
Stuart C. Smith, Associate Director

About the Author

Lawrence O. Picus is professor and chair of the Department of Administration and Policy in the Rossier School of Education at the University of Southern California. He also serves as the director of the Center for Research in Education Finance (CREF), a school-finance research center housed at the Rossier School of Education. CREF research focuses on issues of school finance and productivity. His current research interests focus on adequacy and equity in school finance as well as efficiency and productivity in the provision of educational programs for K-12 school children. Recent work has also included analyses of fiscal implications of vouchers and charter schools.

Picus is the coauthor of *School Finance: A Policy Perspective,* 2nd edition (McGraw-Hill, 2000), with Allan Odden, and of *Principles of School Business Administration* (ASBO, 1995) with R. Craig Wood, David Thompson, and Don I. Tharpe. In addition, he is the senior editor of the 1995 yearbook of the American Education Finance Association, *Where Does the Money Go? Resource Allocation in Elementary and Secondary Schools* (Corwin, 1995). He has published numerous articles in professional journals as well.

In his role with CREF, Picus is involved with studies of how educational resources are allocated and used in schools across the United States. He has also conducted studies of the impact of incentives on school-district performance.

Picus maintains close contact with the superintendents and chief business officers of school districts throughout California and the nation, and is a member of a number of professional organizations dedicated to improving school-district management.

Picus is past-president of the American Education Finance Association. He is a member of the Editorial Advisory Committee of the Association of School Business Officials, International, and he has served as a consultant to the National Education Association, American Federation of Teachers, the National Center for Education Statistics, WestEd, and the states of Washington, Vermont, Oregon, Wyoming, South Carolina, Louisiana, and Arkansas.

Prior to coming to USC, Picus spent four years at the RAND Corporation where he earned a Ph.D. in Public Policy Analysis. He holds a master's degree in social science from the University of Chicago, and a bachelor's degree in economics from Reed College.

Acknowledgments

Understanding how money impacts student performance is a critical policy issue facing educators today. This volume was developed to summarize what we know to date about this important topic. It represents a compilation of work I have done for a number of years and in a variety of capacities. The opportunity to bring it all together in one place was one I could not refuse.

I would like to thank Stuart Smith, associate director of the ERIC Clearinghouse on Educational Management, for seeking me out and asking me to undertake this work. More importantly, I'd like to thank Stu and his staff for their patience with me as deadlines approached and passed, and for their diligence in reviewing drafts, providing editorial comments, and keeping things moving along.

I would also like to thank my research assistant Stephen Thomas, who helped with earlier drafts of each chapter. His dedication to the task and his suggestions for improvements have made this work substantially better than it otherwise would have been. I would also like to thank Carolyn McLaurine, the administrative coordinator for the Division of Administration and Policy at the Rossier School of Education (which I chair). Her ability to keep the division running smoothly makes it possible for me to engage in interesting projects like this.

I have benefited greatly from the advice of many of my colleagues over the years. Some have commented directly on earlier drafts of the chapters contained herein, while others have helped shape my thinking over the years. Among them are Allan Odden, David Monk, Yasser Nakib, Donald Tetreault, Pete Bylsma, Bill Fowler, and others too numerous to list. The material here is richer thanks to their help. Any errors and omissions are solely my responsibility.

Finally, I'd like to thank my wife Susan Pasternak and my son Matthew. Their patience with the late hours spent working on this book is appreciated. I'd like to be able to promise them that the smell of coffee drifting through the house at 4:00 a.m. is a thing of the past, but all three of us know better than that. Their love and support continues to motivate me in my work.

Lawrence O. Picus
North Hollywood, California
September 27, 2000

Contents

Tables

Figures

Introduction

The nearly 16,000 public school districts in the United States today spend over $300 billion on K-12 education each year (NCES 1999). This large sum represents more than is spent each year by the Department of Defense. Despite this substantial effort, public schools today are often criticized for failing to educate our children adequately. In response, the education community often claims that they do not have enough money to do the job being demanded of them. They argue that with more money, they can do a better job.

Yet the fact is, over the last 40 years, resources for public education have increased dramatically (NCES 1999). Where has this money gone? And has it been spent in ways that lead to improved student performance? Unfortunately, despite substantial research into the topic of how money matters in schools, the answer is still far from clear.

The purpose of this volume is not to resolve the debate over whether money matters, or how it matters. Rather, this volume seeks to put in one place a summary of the research conducted to date on this complex and interesting topic. As the pages that follow show, researchers have not been able to document conclusively that more money will lead to higher student performance. Part of the reason for this absence of certainty is there is not always agreement as to what is meant by improved performance. While most people consider this to mean higher test scores, many economists argue that a better measure of school quality is the future lifetime earnings of the student.

How money is used will also impact its effectiveness. Should it be used to reduce class size (the most consistent use of additional funds in the last 40 years), raise teacher salaries, build new buildings, or provide better professional development opportunities? Or, since much of the research concludes that student socioeconomic status (SES) has the greatest impact on student performance, perhaps additional resources should be devoted to governmental programs outside of education that have as their goal mitigation of the problems created by low SES. These are complex issues for which answers are not readily available because of inadequate data.

The balance of this volume describes the important components of the research on whether, and how, money matters. Chapter 1 begins with a discussion of production functions. Most research on the topic of how money matters falls into the category of a production-function study. Typically these studies attempt to estimate the effect of additional resources on some outcome such as student test scores while controlling for student, school, and district characteristics.

A wide range of dependent and independent variables are used in these studies, and the quality of the research varies tremendously. Moreover, analysts who have reviewed many of the studies come to different conclusions about the effect of additional resources on student outcomes.

Chapter 2 considers a special class of these studies, specifically those that use adult earnings as the measure of student outcomes. Because these incomes cannot be measured for many years, researchers have typically had to use measures of school quality from the past. What is particularly interesting about this line of research is that when state-level measures of school inputs are utilized, there appears to be a positive effect on student outcomes. However, when the data are disaggregated to the school level, this finding seems to disappear.

An important, if shop-worn, point often made in discussions of how money matters is that what may be more important than how much money is available is how that money is spent. Chapter 3 reviews the extensive research that has been conducted, mostly over the last ten years, on how schools and school districts allocate and use the resources available to them.

In chapter 4, the extensive research on the impact of class size on student achievement is the subject of a detailed discussion. This topic is included in the monograph because the single largest expenditure of our public schools is for teachers. Lowering class size is consequently an expensive proposition. Understanding the impact of such reductions on both the budget and student achievement is therefore very important.

One of the problems with all this research is the availability and quality of the data. Chapter 5 provides a discussion of the costs and benefits of collecting school-level and even student-level data from schools and suggests how those data might be used to improve the quality of our research on this topic.

Finally, chapter 6 offers some suggestions for different ways data might be used, and outlines the important policy considerations faced by federal, state, and local officials in determining how to make the use of educational resources more cost-effective.

The research in this field changes on an almost daily basis. It is entirely possible that by the time you read this, new studies will have provided additional insights into how money matters. Let us hope so. Without the continued efforts of dedicated researchers, the answers to these complex questions will continue to elude us.

CHAPTER 1

Does Money Matter?
An Analysis of Production-Function
Research and Findings

$\mathbf{A}$sk most teachers or school administrators if they could do a better job educating children if they had more money, and virtually every one of them will offer a resounding "yes." Ask them what they would do with that money, and their answer is less clear. Many educators do not have a strategic sense of how the money could be used, and more often than not the answer will conflict with what other teachers or administrators say is needed.

Today's school reformers increasingly call for greater productivity in our schools. As Monk (1992) shows, productivity is a difficult concept to apply to a public good like education. Nevertheless, for the purpose of this book, here is a straightforward working definition of *educational productivity*: the improvement of student outcomes with little or no additional financial resources, or a consistent level of student performance at a lower level of spending. Although a simple idea, improvements in student achievement absent large amounts of new money have been relatively rare in public schools in the United States.

One of the difficulties in discussing educational productivity is the many different ways it can be addressed. The first section of this chapter reviews the literature that seeks to answer the question, "Does money matter?"

The second section discusses why it has been difficult in education to identify productive uses of school funds.

The third section considers the use of production functions more generally in trying to ascertain the connection between money and student learning. It explains the equations that are used in production-function research and describes the difficulties commonly encountered with such research.

The Current Debate: Does Money Matter?

One can measure educational productivity through three lenses: efficiency, effectiveness, and equity. *Efficiency* refers to the allocation of resources and their use in schools. Specifically, efficiency concerns revolve around how much money schools have, and how that money is used. *Effectiveness* encompasses the linkage between student outcomes and the level and use of financial resources in the schools. This topic, a matter of considerable debate in educational and economic circles, is the focus of this section. The third approach to measuring productivity is *equity*, the equitable distribution of funds to all children.

Virtually all effectiveness studies rely on an economic method known as the production function. This section begins with a discussion of production functions and how they are used. While this is not necessarily the only way to measure the effectiveness or productivity of a school system, it has been the method most frequently used.

Research Using Production Functions

While interest in the question of whether money matters has always been high, the publication of an article by Hedges, Laine, and Greenwald (1994a) in the April 1994 *Education Researcher* sparked renewed debate over this issue. Prior to publication of this article, the most often cited research in this field was the work of Eric Hanushek (1981, 1986, and 1989). In those articles, as well as his more recent research, Hanushek (1997) argues that there does not appear to be a systematic relationship between the level of funding and student outcomes.

Hanushek has now analyzed 90 different publications, with 377 separate production-function equations. In the summer 1997 issue of *Educational Evaluation and Policy Analysis*, he continues to argue that "these results have a simple interpretation: There is no strong or consistent relationship between school resources and student performance. In other words, there is little reason to be confident that simply adding more resources to schools as currently constituted will yield performance gains among students" (Hanushek 1997, p. 148).

To reach this conclusion, Hanushek followed a process that separates the studies on the basis of the outcome measures employed by the authors, and then looks at the regression results. The regressions use a series of independent or descriptor variables to estimate the value of the dependent or, in this case, outcome variable. The regression estimates the nature of the relationship between the independent variables and the dependent variable, measures the estimated strength of that relationship, and indicates whether the estimate of the effect is statistically significant (whether one can say with some level of confidence that the answer is different from zero).

For example, let's say the researcher is interested in whether more money leads to higher test scores. If the sign on the coefficient of expenditures is positive, the implication is that higher spending leads to higher test scores. However, one needs to be sensitive to the magnitude of that relationship and the confidence one has about that estimate (the statistical significance).

Hanushek, using this same method, divided the results of the 377 equations into 5 categories as follows:

- A positive relationship that is statistically significant
- A positive relationship that is not statistically significant
- A negative relationship that is statistically significant
- A negative relationship that is not statistically significant
- A situation where the direction of the relationship can not be determined

In addition to school expenditures, some of the studies relied on other measures of school district resource allocation; they looked at teacher/pupil ratios,* expenditures for central or school-site administration, teacher education, and teacher experience.

Hanushek analyzed the studies and placed them in one of the five categories based on the estimated effect described above. In looking across studies, at different outcome measures and different types of inputs, Hanushek argues that the variation in findings is such that systematic relationships between money and outcomes have not yet been identified. He states:

> The concern from a policy viewpoint is that nobody can describe when resources will be used effectively and when they will not. In the absence of such a description, providing these general resources to a school implies that sometimes resources might be used effectively, other times they may be applied in ways that are actually damaging, and most of the time no measurable student outcome gains should be expected. (Hanushek 1997, pp. 148-9)

He then suggests that what is needed is to change the incentive structures facing schools so that they are motivated to act in ways that use resources efficiently and that lead to improved student performance.

One of the most interesting findings in Hanushek's (1997) recent work is the impact of aggregation on the results. Studies that use data aggregated to the state level, he found, are far more likely to find statistically significant and positive relationships than are studies that focus on the classroom or school level. What is not clear from his work at this point is whether the aggregation is masking much of the variance that exists (a likely occurrence), or if we simply do not yet have tools that are refined enough to

---

* While it is generally easier to think in terms of a pupil/teacher ratio, the advantage of reversing this ratio and considering a teacher/pupil ratio is to simplify discussion. Typically a lower pupil/teacher ratio is more expensive and considered a positive step toward improving student performance. However, if smaller classes lead to higher student performance, then the relationship between the pupil/teacher ratio and the outcome measure will be negative. If the ratio is reversed, so that it is a teacher/pupil ratio, the higher the teacher/pupil ratio, the smaller the class size. Thus if small class size leads to improved student performance, the sign on the coefficient will be positive.

adequately measure the effects of different inputs at the most disaggregated levels in the system.

Others have looked at the same studies as Hanushek and concluded that they show money does make a difference. Hedges, Laine, and Greenwald (1994a, 1994b; see also Laine, Greenwald, and Hedges 1996; and Greenwald, Hedges, and Laine 1996a, 1996b) conclude that, in fact, money can make a difference. They argue that while in those studies only a minority of relationships indicate a positive, statistically significant relationship, the number with such a relationship exceeds what one would expect to find if the relationship were random. They also point out that one would expect the statistically insignificant studies to be evenly divided between positive and negative effects, yet in this category as many as 70 percent of the relationships between per-pupil expenditures and student performance are positive.

Relying on this and other evidence, Greenwald, Hedges, and Laine (1996a) conclude that school spending and achievement are related. In his rejoinder, Hanushek (1996) argues that while there is evidence that the relationship exists, there is not evidence of a strong or systematic relationship.

A number of other studies have looked at this issue. Ferguson (1991) examined spending and the use of educational resources in Texas. He concluded that "hiring teachers with stronger literacy skills, hiring more teachers (when students-per-teacher exceed 18), retaining experienced teachers, and attracting more teachers with advanced training are all measures that produce higher test scores in exchange for more money" (Ferguson 1991, p. 485).

Ferguson's findings also suggest that the education level of the adults in the community, the racial composition of that community, and the salaries in other districts and alternative occupations affect teachers' selection of districts in which they want to teach. According to Ferguson, this implies that better teachers tend to move to districts with higher socioeconomic characteristics if salaries are equal. If teacher skills and knowledge have an impact on student achievement (and Ferguson, as well as others, suggest that they do), then low socioeconomic areas may have to offer substantially higher salaries to attract and retain high-quality instructors. This finding would help confirm a link between expenditures and student achievement.

In a more recent study, Wenglinsky (1997) used regression analysis of three large national databases to see if expenditures had an impact on student achievement of fourth- and eighth-graders. He found that the impact of spending was in steps or stages. For fourth-graders, Wenglinsky concluded that increased expenditures on instruction and on school district administration increase teacher-student ratios. Increased teacher/student ratios (smaller class sizes) in turn lead to higher achievement in mathematics.

In the eighth grade the process was more complex. Wenglinsky found that increased expenditures on instruction and central administration increase teacher/student ratios (reduce class size). This increased teacher/student ratio led to an improved school environment or climate, and the improved climate and its lack of behavior problems resulted in higher achievement in math.

Equally interesting was Wenglinsky's finding that capital outlay (spending on facility construction and maintenance), school-level administration, and teacher-education levels could not be related to improved student achievement. This is particularly intriguing in light of his finding that increased spending for central or district administration was associated with improved student outcomes. These findings, certain to be controversial, conflict to some extent with the "conventional wisdom" about school administration. Why additional spending on district administration leads to improved teacher/student ratios, whereas that is not the case with school-site administration, is not clear, but this anomaly should be investigated further and considered by school districts when they evaluate the move to site-based management.

In summary, there remains considerable disagreement over the impact of additional resources on educational outcomes of students. The complexity of the educational system, combined with the wide range of outcomes we have established for our schools, and the many alternative approaches we use to fund our schools make it difficult to come to any firm conclusions about whether or not money matters.

Methodological Challenges

One of the problems with all the studies described above is that they do not take into consideration the similarity with which school districts spend the resources available to them. Research by Picus (1993a and 1993b), Picus and Fazal (1996), and Cooper and others (1994) shows resource-allocation patterns across school districts to be remarkably alike, despite differences in total per-pupil spending, student characteristics, and district attributes (see also chapter 4 of this volume).

This does not mean that all children receive the same level of educational services. As Picus and Fazal point out, a district spending $10,000 per pupil and $6,000 per pupil for direct instruction is able to offer smaller classes, better paid and presumably higher quality teachers, and higher quality instructional materials than is a district spending $5,000 per pupil and only $3,000 per pupil for direct instruction.

We do not know what the impact on student performance would be if schools or school districts were to dramatically change the way they spend the resources available to them. In 1992, Odden and Picus suggested that the important message from the research summarized above was that, "if additional education revenues are spent in the same way as current education revenues, student performance increases are unlikely to emerge" (Odden and Picus 1992, p. 281). Therefore, knowing whether high-performing schools use resources differently than other schools would be helpful in resolving the debate over whether money matters.

Nakib (1996) studied the allocation of educational resources by high-performing high schools in Florida and compared those allocation patterns with the way resources were used in the remaining high schools in that state. A total of seven different measures were used to compare student performance. In his findings, Nakib shows that per-pupil spending and per-pupil spending for instruction were not statistically significantly higher in high-performing high schools, largely because of the highly equalized school-funding formula used in Florida. On the other hand, he found that the percentage of expenditures devoted to instruction was lower in the high-performing high schools, implying high-performing high schools may actually spend more money on resources not directly linked to instruction than do other high schools.

Unfortunately, the results of this Florida analysis do little to clarify the debate on whether money matters. The comparison of high-performing high schools with all other high schools in Florida did not show a clear distinction in either the amount of money available or in the way resources are used. As with many other studies, student demographic characteristics were found to have the greatest impact on student performance.

More recently, Odden (1997) has found that the schooling designs developed as part of the New American Schools project have generally led to increased student performance. In each of the seven models he studied, schools are required to make substantial reallocations of resources. They hire fewer aides and teachers with special assignments and instead employ a greater number of regular classroom teachers, thus lowering average class size. In addition, each of the designs requires substantial investments, in both time and money, for professional development. Odden suggests that this can often be funded through elimination of a position through attrition. His optimistic assessment is that for relatively little additional money, schools can fund existing programs and organizational structures that will help them improve student learning.

Why Is Educational Productivity So Elusive?

To date, economists who have attempted to define a production function for education have been largely unsuccessful. Much of the variation in student performance from school to school is related to student characteristics over which schools have no control. Moreover, recent research on educational resource-allocation patterns shows little variation in the way school districts use the funds they have, regardless of per-pupil spending levels (see, for example, Odden, Monk, Nakib, and Picus 1995; Picus and Fazal 1996; and chapter 4 of this volume).

As a result, it has been difficult to identify productive uses of school funds. Before looking at potential ways to break these patterns and improve productivity, it will be helpful to consider some possible reasons these patterns exist.

Financial Organization of School Districts

School districts are typically organized in a top-down fashion, particularly with regard to their fiscal operations. There are a number of reasons for this. First, since schools spend public funds, it is essential that district administrators ensure the money is spent as budgeted and approved by the school board. Considerable expense goes into developing systems that provide this accountability, and it is easier to manage these systems centrally. Moreover, few school-site administrators have the training or desire to become financial managers. Thus school district accounting systems have become highly centralized.

Central fiscal management has its benefits in terms of centralized purchasing and common reporting formats, but it can also reduce local creativity. Most school districts rely on allocation mechanisms to distribute resources to school sites (Hentschke 1986). These mechanisms typically allocate resources such as teachers on a per-pupil basis, and others on either a per-pupil or dollar-per-pupil basis. Depending on the level of detail in a district's system, these allocation mechanisms often leave very little discretionary authority to the school site.

Moreover, most systems do not allow school sites the flexibility to carry over funds if expenditures are below budgeted levels. Although this pattern is changing, to the extent it still exists, schools have little incentive to create long-term plans, and they find themselves better off looking for ways to be sure they have spent all the funds allocated to their site each fiscal year.

School District Budgeting

Budgeting systems also work to limit variation in school spending patterns. Wildavsky (1988) describes public budgeting systems as being incremental. The bulk of a public organization's budget, he notes, is based on the same allocation pattern as the previous year, adjusted for changes in costs due to inflation, salary increases, and price increases. Consequently, changes in spending patterns are unlikely, and when they occur, do so at the margin. That is, it is only after current expenditures are "covered" that new programs are considered, if more money is available.

It is not surprising that school districts have highly incremental budgets. The basic organization of a school district is to put a number of children in a classroom with a teacher. The balance of a school system is designed to support that structure. Depending on local preferences, this includes a central administrative office, school-site administrators, specialists and student-support personnel, aides, and classified staff to handle clerical, custodial, transportation, and other activities. Each year the typical district budgets funds to cover the staff, materials, and fixed costs of the previous year. If funds are inadequate, then it is forced to make reductions, usually at the margin. If new programs are desired, new resources must be found.

Assuming large gains in productivity are desired, it seems that dramatic changes in the ways resources are allocated and used will be needed. Doing so requires breaking the patterns noted above.

Linking Spending to Student Outcomes: Economic Research

Despite these methodological challenges, a considerable number of research studies have examined production functions in education. Such research has taken two approaches to considering whether spending on education leads to improved student outcomes. The first focuses on defining outcomes as student achievement, usually measured through state or local assessment systems, and usually in the form of standardized tests. Most production-function research attempts to link changes in school spending to changes in test scores. Other measures of student performance that are sometimes used include school attendance, dropout rates, college enrollment, and job longevity following high school.

While this approach makes a great deal of sense, many econo-mists argue that the way to measure the impact of additional edu-cational resources is to assess its impact on lifetime earnings. They suggest that education is an investment, and high investment in education will yield higher returns in the form of higher lifetime earnings. In fact, many studies that consider this "human capital" approach find that money makes a difference (see chapter 2).

What Is a Production Function?

As Picus (1997b) points out, nearly all would agree that more money is better than less. Moreover, most would agree that the expenditure of additional funds on education should lead to im-proved student learning. However, there is considerable disagree-ment among researchers whether a statistical link can be found between student outcomes and money (or what money buys, such as lower class size, teacher experience and degrees, and so forth). The single largest expenditure item for a school district is teacher compensation (salary and benefits). So, for example, for a district of a given size, the more money or revenue available to the sys-tem, the more teachers it can hire and the smaller the average class size will be.

Production functions are an economic tool used to measure the contribution of individual inputs to the output of some prod-uct. In simple terms, a production function takes the following form:

(1) $O = f(K,L)$

Where:

O = some measurable output
K = Capital or nonlabor inputs to the production process
L = Labor

By estimating equations that include these variables, as well as other variables that control for exogenous factors known to affect the production process, it is possible to predict the impact that the application of additional units of labor and capital will have on the number of units of output produced.

This concept can be applied to education as well.* For example, it is possible to estimate an educational production function with the following form:

(2) P = f(R,S,D)

Where:

P = A measure of student performance
R = A measure of resources available to students in the school or district
S = A vector of student characteristics
D = A vector of district and school characteristics

One possible measure of R would be the pupil-teacher ratio at a school or school district. In fact, the pupil-teacher ratio is in many ways a good choice for this particular variable as it provides a proxy for the level of resources available for children (that is, it is highly correlated with per-pupil spending), and it is a proxy for class size.

Difficulties with the Educational Production-Function Research

There are substantial methodological difficulties with estimating equations of the form presented above. First and foremost is reaching agreement on the proper measure of student performance to serve as the outcome indicator. Although there is considerable discussion about this in the education community, in recent years, the policy community—as well as most educators—have focused on the results of standardized tests as the outcome measure. The studies described earlier in this chapter generally follow this trend.

There are a number of other methodological problems to consider. There is substantial evidence that children from minority backgrounds, children from low-income families, children who do not speak English as their first language, and children with disabilities do not do as well in school as other children. Therefore, if our model is to identify the impact that smaller classes

---

* For a more detailed description of production functions as they apply to education, see Monk (1990).

have on student performance, it is necessary to control for differences in student characteristics. Unfortunately, it is often difficult to collect these data in ways that facilitate the estimation of a production function.

For example, it is often possible to collect data on student performance and student characteristics at the individual student level. However, other data related to school or district characteristics may be available only at the district level. This is often the case with fiscal data such as per-pupil expenditures and even pupil-teacher ratios. As a result, the regression equations contain variables with varying levels of precision. Unfortunately, the accuracy of the estimates of the impact of resources on student performance is only as good as the lowest level of precision. This is often the district-level fiscal or resource data that are of interest to the researcher. There are statistical techniques to minimize this problem, in particular, Hierarchical Linear Modeling (HLM). However, many of the early studies on the effect of school resources did not use this tool.

Another problem is that most education production-function studies rely on cross-sectional data. This approach allows for a snapshot of one point in time. Yet many of the student characteristic and schooling variables used in these equations are subject to substantial change over time. Thus it is not clear that reliance on a one-time measure of these characteristics will adequately control for their effects on student performance. Longitudinal data sets, which would resolve many of these problems, are expensive to collect, and few are available to researchers today.

In addition, there are substantial problems with the inputs actually measured for this research. The pupil-teacher ratio is often used as a proxy for class size. Picus (1994b) shows that there is considerable variation between the computed pupil-teacher ratio in a district or school and teachers' self-reported class size. While self-reported class size averaged 50 percent larger than the computed pupil-teacher ratio, this figure ranged widely from one or two students more than the computed ratio to more than double that figure. Thus, if one is trying to estimate the effect of class size on student performance in a school or district, the pupil-teacher ratio may not accurately reflect either the class size or the variation that exists in the number of students each teacher sees in a day.

A final problem with this research is that it is generally impossible to establish a true experimental design with both an experimental group and a control group. Instead, student performance at a given grade level before class size is reduced is compared with student performance at that grade level following the implementation of the treatment, in this case the smaller class size. This too reduces the confidence with which one can make statements about the relationship between class size and student performance.

Summary

Production-function research has been used extensively to try to understand whether and how money matters. To date, the research findings have been mixed. This does not imply that money does not matter, only that when using this economic technique, we have yet to conclusively find how it matters. This is not, however, the only approach to assessing the impact of resources on educational outcomes.

In the chapters that follow, other approaches are considered and evaluated. What this discussion shows is that the relationship between money and student learning is not clear cut, but rather is influenced by a wide range of factors in our schools. Understanding the impact of these factors on students, teachers, and other participants in the educational process will help further our ability to learn the best ways to ensure that the money we spend on schools leads to improved student outcomes.

CHAPTER 2

Linking School Resources to Adult Earnings

Chapter 1 focused on the most common approach to understanding the impact of school resources on student achievement, the production function. Several of the chapters that follow look closely at a number of individual resources that educational decision-makers can control in varying degrees to improve student learning; for example, policymakers can reduce class size, add more teacher training, and in other ways adjust how resources are used.

This chapter looks at an alternative specification for determining how money might matter. Specifically, it examines the economic literature to find evidence on how inputs to schooling influence adult earnings.

This line of reasoning is derived from the substantial literature on human-capital theory, which suggests that investments in education lead to improvements in economic productivity generally, and to higher earnings for individuals who "invest" in that education. (For an excellent summary of the literature on human-capital theory, see Sweetland 1996). While it is clear that individual investment in schooling (for example, staying in school longer) brings personal benefits in terms of higher earnings, there is less evidence that public investment in additional school resources generally will lead to higher adult earnings for those students who benefit from that greater public investment. This chapter examines the human-capital literature with a focus on how investments in education influence long-term adult earnings.

The best-known studies on the impact of school quality on lifetime earnings were conducted by Card and Kruger (1992a, 1992b, 1995, and 1996) and Julian Betts (1995 and 1996). Like the discussion of production functions in chapter 1, the evidence presented by these researchers is not conclusive. Additional work by Heckman, Layne-Farrar, and Todd (1996) has provided more insight into this important question, but again, more research is needed before statistical evidence will permit us to conclude that adult earnings are positively correlated with measures of school quality.

This chapter is divided into four sections. The first considers the evidence developed by Card and Krueger that suggests school quality has positive effects on adult earnings. The second section looks closely at the work of Julian Betts and his finding that as data are disaggregated from state-level variables to district- and eventually school-level variables, the relationship seems to weaken and even disappear. Then the studies of Heckman, Layne-Farrar, and Todd are reviewed. In the last section, the current "state-of-the-art" in this type of analysis is summarized.

School Quality Does Matter

Despite the substantial literature on the impact of investment in education on individual earnings and on economic productivity, little research has been conducted on the effect of measures of school quality on adult earnings or economic productivity. The reason for this has to do largely with the difficulty of obtaining adequate data.

Although census data provide estimates of annual earnings for cohorts of individuals over time, data on measures of school quality are not as reliable. Examples of school-quality measures for which data might be available include expenditures per pupil, pupil-teacher ratios, and average teacher salaries. The problem is finding comparable data on these measures over long periods. State and federal data-collection systems have changed over time as a result of both efforts to improve data quality and budgetary conditions that led to variations in the amount and quality of data collected. Moreover, data on where individuals went to school are often not available, making it hard to link earnings to measures of school quality.

Despite these difficulties, Card and Krueger (1992a and 1992b) conducted a comprehensive analysis of the impact of school quality on adult earnings. Card and Krueger suggested that school quality could influence adult earnings in two ways. First, they theorized that the benefits from higher quality schools would translate into greater learning and hence the ability to earn more income over an individual's lifetime. Second, they suggested that high-quality schools would induce more students to stay in school for a longer time, leading both to higher earnings directly and to a higher probability that the students will attend college and reap the additional gains provided by college studies.

Card and Krueger (1996) analyzed the literature on this issue, comparing the results of 24 estimates of the effect of school quality on adult earnings contained in 11 different studies. They classify the studies into four types as follows:

1. Studies that assume additional years of schooling affect the starting income of individuals whose income then grows at the same rate as does the income of individuals with less schooling (the intercept in regressions estimating the impact of school quality on earnings).

2. Studies that assume additional years of schooling affect both the starting income and the rate at which income grows in the future (both the intercept and the slope).

3. Studies that focus on the impact of school quality on the difference in growth of income (the slope only).

4. A model that attempts to estimate the overall effect of added school resources on adult earnings independent of school attainment. This model attempts to estimate the direct effects of resources on the return to schooling, and the indirect effect of students remaining longer in high-quality schools.

Card and Krueger's (1996) analysis indicated that all the 24 studies fell into either model 1 or model 2, and that all of them show a positive effect of spending on adult earnings.

Card and Krueger's own analysis is based on the use of state-level indicators of school quality. They develop panel data with information on per-pupil spending and pupil-teacher ratios from the 50 states over time. These data are used as measures of school quality and included as independent variables in their equations modeling adult earnings. They conclude from both their review of the literature and from their own analysis that additional resources devoted to schools in the form of higher per-pupil spending and lower pupil-teacher ratios increase the return from an added year of schooling, and that those additional resources encourage students to stay in school longer than they otherwise would do (Burtless 1996).

As part of this work, Card and Krueger also looked at the evidence on the impact of school spending on adult earnings of African-Americans educated in segregated schools. Card and Krueger compared adult earnings of African-American males educated in segregated schools in different states (where different levels of resources were available to African-American children) who moved to, and worked in, other states. Two findings emerge from this analysis. They found that individuals from states that provided more resources had higher adult earnings. They also found that as the effects of segregation ended in more recent years, the gap in earnings between African-Americans and whites has narrowed somewhat.

The overall conclusion of Card and Kruger—and of others using similar methods—seems to be that higher quality schools, as measured by things like spending and pupil-teacher ratio, appear to lead to higher overall earnings for adult graduates of those schools. This earnings differential appears to be composed of two parts, one a direct return due to the higher skills obtained from that quality education, and an indirect return because students in higher quality schools tend to stay in school longer, leading to greater adult earnings.

Do School Inputs Really Matter?

In his analysis of the data on this topic, Julian Betts (1996) reaches a conclusion that differs from Card and Kruger's. Betts reviewed 23 studies that examined the link between school inputs and students' earnings as adults. He concluded that almost all the studies using state-level average inputs found that increases in school spending lead to improvements in earnings. He determined that in a slight majority of the studies using average inputs at the level of the school district, the same result was obtained.

When Betts looked at studies that considered school-level data, however, not one of them found a relationship between spending and future earnings. In other words, to quote Burtless (1996, p. 33), "If inputs are measured using statewide or districtwide averages, there is a better chance that the study will find a statistically significant effect of school expenditures."

Betts (1996) found this general pattern was the same for most other school inputs. The higher the level used to measure inputs (state level being the highest), the greater the likelihood that a statistically significant relationship between inputs and earnings will be found. Further, Betts found that inputs that seem effective when measured at the state level are often insignificantly related to earnings when the input is measured for the actual school attended.

Another pattern identified by Betts is that in studies of students who were in elementary school prior to 1960, school inputs are linked to adult earnings, whereas studies of children in elementary school after 1960 generally find little evidence of such a link. He also found that studies of individuals who are 32 or younger typically don't find a statistically significant impact, whereas studies that looked at individuals who are over 30 almost always found that school resources were significantly linked to adult earnings.

Betts goes on to estimate the internal rate of return to making investments in improved school quality. His estimate of 2.35 percent is very low, despite a set of assumptions that seem largely favorable to such investment. Betts points out that this low rate of return does not particularly favor additional investments in school inputs. Moreover, the return to investment of, say, lower pupil/teacher ratios in elementary school is not likely to occur for many years. This estimate is considerably lower than most estimates of the rate of return to an additional year of schooling, which typically range from 5 to 12 percent (Sweetland 1996).

Missing from Betts' calculations is an estimate of the social benefits from education that certainly exist.

There are a number of potential explanations for the findings that, over time, the link between school inputs and future earnings has been more difficult to establish. One possible explanation is that as the level of resources for school has increased over time (see Odden and Picus 2000 and NCES 1989, 1993, 1996, 1997, and 1998 for evidence of this), the marginal benefit of the additional resources declines with the rise in the average level of inputs. Betts argues that the variation in the data is not large enough to reach such a conclusion with great confidence.

Burtless (1996) suggests that other changes in school organization such as increased bureaucratization and teacher unionization may have made it more difficult to link additional resources to improved outcomes, because additional funds would be directed to things that met the interests of administrators and teachers rather than things that had the greatest impact on learning. Again, there is little evidence to substantiate or deny this hypothesis.

Another possible reason for later studies finding a weaker link between school inputs and adult earnings is that, over time, differences in per-pupil expenditures have been reduced, making it harder to estimate the effects of such differences on outcomes. However, these differences remain substantial today (Odden and Picus 2000) and seem to vary sufficiently to allow significant findings.

Card and Krueger also suggested that additional school inputs will induce students to stay in school longer, and that additional school attendance will lead to improved adult earnings. In reviewing studies that consider this question specifically, Betts (1996) found that the effects of additional inputs on student attainment are stronger in state-level studies and virtually disappear in studies relying on school-level data. As in the case of the direct return, Betts concludes that the use of school-level data weakens the finding of a link between additional school inputs and future earnings.

Do Inputs Matter?

Like the debate over production functions described in chapter 1, the evidence presented in this chapter thus far suggests that there is no simple yes or no answer to the question of whether additional investment in school quality will lead to improved lifetime earnings. Heckman, Layne-Farrar, and Todd (1996) consider the issue further.

They begin by pointing out that the earliest studies of this question (see, for example, Johnson and Stafford 1973) assumed that the difference in earnings that resulted from higher school quality—as measured by school inputs—was constant for every level of school attainment. That is, if earnings were plotted as a function of school attainment for a state with high investment and for a state with low investment, the lines would be parallel, with earnings for every level of school attainment higher for the state with the greater investment.

Later studies assumed that these lines are not parallel, but rather the size of the benefit, as measured by lifetime earnings, increases as years of schooling increase. In this case, the slope of the line plotted to represent earnings as a function of years of schooling would be steeper for the high-investment state than for the low-investment state. This is essentially the method used by Card and Krueger (1992a).

In more technical terms, the first model assumes that the intercept of the two plots differs and that the slope is the same. The second model assumes that the intercept is the same, but the slope is steeper for the state with greater investment in educational inputs. Heckman, Layne-Farrar, and Todd (1996) use a model that assumes both the intercepts and slopes of the two lines differ. They hypothesize that the intercept for the high-investment state is higher than for the low-investment state, and that the slope of the line plotted is steeper. In other words, there is an initial advantage to going to school in a state that spends more per pupil on education, and that the longer one stays in school, the greater that advantage becomes as measured by future earnings.

Heckman, Layne-Farrar, and Todd (1996) also relax the assumption that the relationship between earnings and school inputs is linear. They suggest that there very likely are "sheepskin" effects. That is, the return to a high school or a college diploma exceeds the value of an additional year of schooling alone. In other words, future earnings for a student who completes the 12th grade and earns a high-school diploma are greater than the additional earnings garnered for completion of the 11th grade. Similarly, the gain from completing the fourth year of college and earning a degree are greater than the gain from completing the second or third year of college. This assumption can be tested by relaxing the assumption that the relationship between earnings and school inputs is linear.

Heckman, Layne-Farrar, and Todd (1996) reestimated Card and Krueger's model using the same data, supplemented with data from later census files. The result of this work is to confirm Card and Krueger's earlier findings that there is a substantial gain in adult earnings in response to investments in school quality. They find these results are stronger using the 1990 census than the 1980 census, which was used by Card and Krueger.

Heckman, Layne-Farrar, and Todd (1996) then relaxed the assumption that the relationship between school inputs and earnings is linear and reestimated the model. When they did this, they found the so-called sheepskin effects to be very strong. In fact, they found that for workers who did not complete college, elementary and high-school resources have little impact on earnings. Such investments in K-12 school quality only appear to have an effect on college graduates.

Summary

Not surprisingly, the debate over the effect of resources on student outcomes has not reached a final conclusion, even when the outcome shifts from student test scores to students' future lifetime earnings. In many ways, using lifetime earnings to measure the value of additional investments in education is an attractive alternative to reliance on student achievement. The focus on earnings does not limit the study to the immediate effects of school inputs, but rather captures a broader measure of what a student is able to get out of his or her education. In that regard, it is an attractive alternative to the standardized test results that are commonly used to estimate school effects.

The problem with using earnings as a measure of school effectiveness is that it takes a long time to see the results of such investments. In a time of instant policy analysis, time lags that last for decades are probably unacceptable to policymakers. Thus, to the extent that reliance on future earnings is the focus of attempts to measure the impact of investments in education, the policy community is likely to grow impatient.

There is, however, a more promising alternative in the literature. Specifically, limited evidence suggests that investments in improved school quality will help keep students in school longer. Given the ample evidence that additional schooling will lead to greater lifetime earnings, it seems important to look more closely at this issue. Moreover, the time lag associated with measurement of future earnings disappears. Policy analysts will be able to measure the impact of investments in schooling on student attainment almost immediately. Although the impact of investment in school quality measured in this manner is indirect, rather than direct, the immediacy of the results makes such information more useful to policymakers.

Estimating the impact of additional investment in education on future lifetime earnings is an attractive alternative to the current emphasis on test results. Limiting the analysis only to individual earnings, however, may underestimate the value of the investment, because it ignores the social benefits of education. (Basing the estimate on student test results alone suffers from the same problem.)

Moreover, the limited research that has been conducted to date seems to show that the relationship weakens as we disaggregate data to smaller units of analysis, that is, the school. Additional research is needed to understand why this occurs.

More important, however, is the need to understand the impact of this investment on years of schooling. If spending money to improve our schools will keep students in schools longer, and additional years of schooling lead to improved lifetime earnings, then the investment may well be worthwhile.

What is important to consider is how those additional funds should be spent. If the goal were to keep students in school longer, should school officials use new funds to purchase the things schools typically use today, or are there other things that would be more likely to keep students in school? And, if schools figured out what would keep students in school longer, would the long-term result be improved earnings for those newly retained students? These are complex questions for which more research and analysis are needed. In particular, what if very different inputs were needed to retain large numbers of students? Would we be willing to make that investment on the assumption that it would benefit students in the long run?

CHAPTER 3

Resource Allocation

Distributing dollars to districts in equitable ways is a first step in providing educational resources for the purposes of educating children. Interdistrict resource allocation has dominated school finance for years. However, tangible methods of productively using those resources in districts, schools, and classrooms should be the focus of the research community.

There is considerable misinformation about how schools use money. Former U.S. Secretary of Education William Bennett and many others have implied that too much money is used for administration, popularizing the term the "administrative blob."

This chapter discusses the appropriation of dollars once they reach districts. The questions that require answers are:

- Where did the money go? To instruction? To regular classroom teachers? To specialist teachers working outside the regular classroom? To administration and the alleged administrative "blob"? To support services? To raise teachers' salaries? To lower class size? To lengthen the school day or year? To "overhead"?

- How was it used? To increase instruction in the regular program? To boost instruction in the core academic programs? To teach more curriculum content? To improve mathematics and science, in which the country still wants to improve student performance? To provide services for special-needs students? And does resource use differ across elementary, middle, and high schools?

- What impact did it have on student achievement? How do resource allocation and use patterns relate to student per-

This chapter draws heavily from Odden and Picus (2000), and from Odden, Monk, Nakib, and Picus (1995).

formance? Have these patterns changed toward patterns that produce more learning? Are the linkages different at the elementary, middle, and high school levels?

Although there is still more work to be done, school finance as a field of study is slowly beginning to provide answers to these questions.

The focus of research in the 1990s shifted as researchers sought to acquire data on resource allocation and use at the school and classroom levels. This shift occurred because schools and classrooms are the "production units" in education. As such, the following types of data need to be collected at each level (elementary, middle, and high school) of schooling.

- Expenditure by program—the regular instruction program; programs for special-needs students such as compensatory, bilingual, and special education; administration; staff development; and instructional materials

- Expenditures by content area—mathematics, language arts (reading in elementary schools), science, history/social science, foreign language, art, music, and physical education

- Interrelationships among these expenditure patterns

- Relationships of these expenditure patterns to student performance

The field of school finance is far from having this knowledge. At present, few states report expenditures by program area with their current accounting systems, and only Florida, Ohio, and Texas can report expenditure and staffing data by site.

Nevertheless, these data are the minimum needed to address productivity questions. Policymakers want to know where new money goes, what resources—especially instructional and curriculum resources—it buys, and what impact those resources have on student performance. These are very reasonable questions.

Further, the total expenditure by level for elementary, middle, and high schools across the United States and within most of the 50 states is not known. Data are not systematically collected by school level (Busch and Odden 1997). This is an important observation because altering resource-use patterns at the school site might be the most promising way to improve productivity of the education system. However, school-finance reformers who advocate this method of reform cannot alter resource-use patterns efficiently without collecting total expenditure by levels. Also, since investments in early education seem to have high payoffs in terms of student learning, perhaps one reason student achievement is low is that our nation underinvests in education in the early years, particularly pre-K and K-3, and overinvests in education at the secondary and postsecondary levels.

This chapter provides a brief overview of how education dollars are used. The first section describes expenditures by function and staffing patterns on a national and statewide basis. Section two discusses how expenditure and use patterns vary across districts within a state, especially across different spending levels. The final section describes information about expenditures at the site level. (See chapter 5 for a discussion of the challenges associated with formally collecting resource data at the school-site level.)

Resource-Use Patterns at the National and State Levels

All 50 states collect fiscal data from their school districts. These data include information on district revenues and expenditures, and on district employees. The revenue data generally contain information on the sources and amounts of revenue received by each school district. Expenditure data are most frequently collected by object of expenditure, divided into categories such as professional salaries, classified salaries, employee benefits, materials and supplies, and capital expenditures. States now also collect expenditure data by broad program area or function such as instruction, administration, transportation, plant operation and maintenance, and debt service.

Staffing data usually specify the number of licensed staff employed by each district, and contain information on job title such as teacher, administrator, principal, librarian, counselor, and so forth. Also, some states maintain databases with information on instructional aides. In a few states, data on teacher credentials and/ or teaching assignments are also available.

Analysis of these data provides a beginning toward knowing how money is used, but the results are several steps removed from the data needed to answer important productivity issues. Nevertheless, these data provide a starting point for identifying how districts use money.

Expenditures by Function

Annually, the National Center for Education Statistics (NCES) provides nationwide and individual state data on expenditures by function. Prior to 1990, the definitions for functional categories differed across states, and thus NCES was able to report expenditures across only a few very broad functional categories.

Table 3.1 provides data on expenditures by function at the national level from 1920 to 1980. Two points should be noted about the data in this table. First, the distribution of expenditures by function changed over these 60 years. The data show that the percentage spent on instruction declined during the first three decades, and that the percentage spent on operation, maintenance, and fixed charges (benefits) increased over this period. Second, the percentage spent on instruction remained about the same from 1950 onward. Since the percentages are related to total expenditures, which include capital as well as current expenditures, the amount spent on instruction as a percentage of current expenses needs to be calculated. The figure would be 60.8 percent for 1980, a figure quite close to the percentage spent on instruction today.

During the late 1980s and early 1990s, the National Center for Education Statistics inaugurated a project to collect more detailed expenditure data that also were comparable across states. During this process NCES also changed somewhat the categories of data collected. Table 3.2 displays national data on expenditures by function for both 1990-91 and 1994-95. The data show that instructional expenditures continued to compose about 61 percent of the operating budget, rising slightly from 60.5 percent in 1991 to 61.7 percent in 1995. The data also show what have become typical expenditure distributional patterns: about 10 percent for student and instructional support, 3 percent for district

Table 3.1

PERCENTAGE DISTRIBUTION OF EXPENDITURES BY FUNCTION, 1920 TO 1980

	1920	1930	1940	1950	1960	1970	1980
Total expenditures, all schools	100.0	100.0	100.0	100.0	100.0	100.0	100.0
Current expenditures, all schools	83.4	80.0	83.4	80.9	79.8	85.7	91.2
Public elementary & secondary schools	83.1	79.6	82.8	80.3	79.0	84.1	90.6
Administration	3.5	3.4	3.9	3.8	3.4	3.9	4.4
Instruction	61.0	56.9	59.9	53.3	53.5	57.2	55.5
Plant operation	11.2	9.3	8.3	7.3	6.9	6.2	—
Plant maintenance	2.9	3.4	3.1	3.7	2.7	2.4	10.2
Fixed charges	0.9	2.2	2.1	4.5	5.8	8.0	12.3
Other school services*	3.5	4.4	5.5	7.7	6.6	6.3	8.3
Summer Schools	(**)	(**)	(**)	(**)	0.1	0.3	(****)
Adult Education**	0.3	0.4	0.6	0.6	0.2	0.3	—
Community Colleges	(**)	(**)	(**)	(**)	0.2	0.3	—
Community Services	(*)	(*)	(*)	(*)	0.4	0.6	0.6
Capital outlay***	14.8	16.0	11.0	17.4	17.0	11.5	6.8
Interest on school debt	1.8	4.0	5.6	1.7	3.1	2.9	2.0

— Data not available

Note: Beginning in 1959-60, includes Alaska and Hawaii. Because of rounding, details may not add to totals.

* Prior to 1959-60, items included under "other school services" were listed under "auxiliary services," a more comprehensive classification which also included community services.

** Prior to 1959-60, data shown for adult education represent combined expenditures for adult education, summer schools, and community colleges.

*** Prior to 1969-70, excludes capital outlay by state and local school housing authorities.

****Less than 0.05 percent.

Source: NCES (1989), p. 151.

Table 3.2

CURRENT EXPENDITURES BY FUNCTION FOR
THE UNITED STATES,
1991-1995

| | *Percent* | |
Current Expenditures	1990-91	1994-95
Instruction	60.5	61.7
Instructional Support	4.2	4.0
Student Support	6.9	6.1
District Administration	2.9	2.4
School Administration	5.8	5.8
Operation and Maintenance	10.5	10.7
Student Transportation	4.3	4.1
Food	4.2	4.2
Other	0.5	0.3

Totals may not equal 100 percent due to rounding.
Source: NCES (1998), p. 162

administration, 6 percent for site administration, 10 percent for operations and maintenance, and about 10 percent for transportation, food, and other services.

Individual state patterns differ but not dramatically from this national average. Table 3.3 lists the percentages spent on instruction by several states. Hawaii, for example, with the highest state role in funding schools, spent 61.9 percent on instruction, very close to the national average of 61.7 percent. On the other hand, New Hampshire, which has the largest local and smallest state role in funding public education, spent 64.4 percent on instruction, slightly above the national average. The other states listed spent just under or just over the national average. The data show that states quite consistently spend just over 60 percent of their

Table 3.3

INSTRUCTIONAL EXPENDITURES FOR SELECTED STATES,
1994-95

	Instruction as Percentage of Current Operating Expenses
California	60.0
Hawaii	61.9
Kentucky	60.0
New Hampshire	64.4
New Jersey	60.0
Texas	61.2
Utah	67.3
Wisconsin	63.5
United States	61.7

Source: NCES (1998).

current operating education budget on instruction, which are the expenditures that provide direct teaching services to students.

Staffing Patterns

Translating these broad expenditures into staffing patterns is the next step toward analyzing what happens to the education dollar. Table 3.4 presents national data on the distribution of school district staff by staffing category from fall 1960 to fall 1995.

Administrators do not appear to represent a large portion of the total. Central-office administrators totaled just 1.7 percent of total staff in 1995 and site administrators just 2.4 percent. Combined, administrators composed just 4.1 percent of all staff, a fairly small percentage, given the charges that the education system spends so much on administration.

Table 3.4

STAFF EMPLOYED IN THE PUBLIC SCHOOLS, 1960 TO 1995
(Percentage Distribution)

	1960	1970	1980	1990	1995
District Administrators	2.0	1.9	1.9	1.7	1.7
Instructional Staff	69.8	68.0	68.6	67.9	67.1
Site Administrators	3.0	2.7	2.6	2.8	2.4
Teachers	64.8	60.0	52.4	53.4	52.0
Teacher Aides	—	1.7	7.8	8.8	9.9
Counselors	0.8	1.7	1.8	1.8	1.8
Librarians	0.8	1.3	1.2	1.1	1.0
Support Staff	28.1	30.1	29.5	30.4	31.2

Source: NCES (1998), p. 89.

Instructional staff dropped from 69.8 percent in 1960 to 67.1 percent in 1997. But this small decline masked larger changes in the composition of instructional staff. Although not shown in the table, teachers constituted 74.1 percent of total staff in 1950. The table shows that the percentage of teachers declined to 64.8 percent in 1960 and then to only 52.0 percent in 1995. At the same time, the percentage of instructional aides rose from almost zero in 1960 to 9.9 percent in 1995.

Similarly, the percentage of support staff also rose over this period, from 28.2 percent in 1960 to 31.2 percent in 1995. These numbers show that about one-third of the total staff in education perform nonadministrative roles, such as secretaries and operation, maintenance, and transportation personnel. When policymakers and local taxpayers wonder why only 60 percent of expenditures are spent on instruction, one answer is that operations, maintenance, transportation, and district administration accounts for nearly a third of public school expenditures.

The bottom line, though, is that the percentage of teachers has dropped nearly 33 percent in the latter half of the 20th century. They have been "replaced" by instructional aides, pupil support staff, and as discussed below, by specialist teachers within schools but who do not teach in regular classrooms. The policy and productivity issue is whether this use of resources is the most effective.

These broad staffing categories are at best indirect indicators of how school funds are spent. Table 3.5 disaggregates the figures a little more and shows the distribution of secondary teachers by content area in 1981, 1986, and 1996. These figures give some indication of the amount spent by content area, important information in an era when improved student performance in the core academic content areas is a national priority.

In 1981, 65.2 percent of secondary teachers were in the core academic areas of English, mathematics, science, social studies, and foreign language. That increased to 69.3 percent in 1986 and to 72.3 percent in 1996. The declines occurred primarily in home economics, industrial arts, and business education. The numbers suggest that academics "won" and vocational education "lost" in resource shifts reflected by the subject-area licenses of secondary teachers in the years following the publication of *A Nation at Risk* (NCEEE 1983), the report that spawned the education-reform movement of the 1980s and 1990s. While not definitive, the numbers indicate that resource allocations shifted in line with reform expectations. Unfortunately, similar staffing data are not available for elementary and middle schools.

In the late 1980s, NCES began a comprehensive School and Staffing Survey (SASS) to produce more detailed information on how schools and classrooms are staffed across the country. The data became available in 1990 and can be used in future analyses to identify staffing patterns by state, level of education, primary field assignment, and a variety of teacher characteristics, such as sex, race, ethnic origin, age, marital status, level of education, major assignment field, and area in which licensed. Table 3.6 indicates the distribution of teachers by primary assignment field for the overall SASS sample for both elementary and secondary

Table 3.5

SECONDARY TEACHERS BY CONTENT AREA, 1981, 1986, and 1996

	Percent of Total		
Subject	*1981*	*1986*	*1996*
Agriculture	1.1	.06	0.5
Art	3.1	1.5	3.3
Business Education	6.2	6.5	4.1
English	23.8	21.8	23.9
Foreign Language	2.8	3.7	5.2
Health/PE	6.5	5.6	5.9
Home Economics	3.6	2.6	2.2
Industrial Arts	5.2	2.2	0.5
Mathematics	15.3	19.2	17.2
Music	3.7	4.8	4.3
Science	12.1	11.0	12.6
Social Studies	11.2	13.6	13.4
Special Education	2.1	3.5	1.7
Other	3.3	3.4	5.2
Total	995,000	970,000	1,049,000

Source: NCES (1989), p. 73; NCES (1998), p.80

schools. The data in this table show the subjects teachers actually taught, whereas the data in the previous table indicate the licenses that teachers held.

The data in table 3.6 show that the majority of teachers in elementary schools were elementary school generalists, with very few having content-specific assignments. Also, 13.4 percent of

Table 3.6

ELEMENTARY AND SECONDARY TEACHERS
BY PRIMARY ASSIGNMENT FIELD
1987-88

	Percent of Total	
Primary Assignment Field	Elementary	Secondary
English/Language Arts	1.3	15.5
Mathematics	1.3	13.8
Social Studies	0.8	12.0
Science	0.8	11.9
General Elementary, Prekindergarten & Kindergarten	78.1	
Special Education	13.4	9.0
Foreign Language	0.2	3.7
Art/Music	2.0	7.0
Vocational Education	0.2	18.8
Physical Education	2.1	8.3

Source: Bobbitt and McMillan (1990).

elementary teachers were in special education. At the secondary level, 56.9 percent of the teachers in the sample had assignments in the academic core areas of English/language arts, mathematics, social studies, science, and foreign language, somewhat below the figures in the preceding table. Indeed, though only 9.0 percent of secondary teachers were licensed in vocational education, close to 18.8 were actually teaching courses in vocational education.

These nationwide data provide the beginnings of detailed information on staffing patterns in schools, but future analyses disaggregating the data to local and school levels would provide even more useful information on how dollars are transformed into staffing patterns.

Resource-Use Patterns
at the District Level

Since education services are organized by the local education system—school districts—and provided in schools and classrooms, statewide expenditure patterns need to be disaggregated to these lower levels. This section first analyzes several studies of expenditure patterns across districts within a state and then reviews the research on how *districts* use new money.

Expenditure Patterns Across Districts Within a State

Research is showing that most districts follow relatively standard practices in using education resources. The major portion of the education budget is spent on instruction, but a large portion of these instructional expenditures today is spent outside the regular classroom on services for special-needs students. This strategy reflects a system characterized by good values but unimpressive results, because the typical "pullout" strategy of providing extra services has not had much positive impact on those students' learning. Districts also provide a host of noneducation services. Districts operate buses, heat and clean buildings, serve meals, and administer a complex system. The result is that only a small portion of the education dollar is spent on regular-education instruction.

Table 3.7 draws from studies of district-level expenditure patterns in three major states: Florida, California, and New York (Monk, Roellke, and Brent 1996; Nakib 1996; Picus, Tetreault, and Murphy 1996). The data show, not surprisingly, that districts spend about 60 percent on instruction, which includes both regular-education instruction in mathematics, language arts, writing, history, and science, as well as instruction for students with special needs such as the disabled. The proportion spent on instruction (60 percent) is quite consistent across the states and squares with the figure from national studies. These studies also examined the spending patterns across a number of different district characteristics, including spending level, rural and urban location, high and low percentages of minority students, as well as

Table 3.7

CURRENT EXPENDITURES BY FUNCTION (PERCENT)
ACROSS THE NATION AND IN CALIFORNIA,
FLORIDA, AND NEW YORK

Expenditure Function	Nation (NCES)	California*	Florida	New York
Instruction	61.2	60.8	58.4	61.8
Instructional Support and Student Services	8.7	7.9	9.9	8.6
Total Administration	8.4	11.4	11.1	10.2
District Administration	(2.6)	(3.2)	(4.4)	(5.7)
School Administration	(5.8)	(8.2)	(6.9)	(4.5)
Operation and Maintenance	10.3	13.4	10.7	9.3
Transportation	4.2	1.5	4.2	6.3
Short Term Capital		0.4	0.3	1.1
Food Services	4.2	4.6	5.2	2.7

*Large unified districts.

Source: Monk, Roellke, and Brent (1996); Nakib (1995); Picus, Tetreault, and Murphy (1996); NCES (1996), Table 160.

students from low-income families, and the patterns were remarkably consistent. The coefficient of variation for percentages spent on instruction was just 10 percent, meaning the proportion varied from about 53 to 66 percent for two-thirds of all districts.

These figures are similar to the findings from other studies of school district expenditures: the Odden, Palaich, and Augenblick (1979) study of New York, two studies of districts in Pennsylvania (Hartman 1988a, 1988b, 1993), and studies by Cooper (1993) and Speakman, Cooper, Holsomback, May, and Sampieri (1993) in New York.

Table 3.8 displays these data by high, medium, and low levels of operating spending levels for New York for the 1977-78 school

Table 3.8

EXPENDITURES BY FUNCTION BY LEVEL OF
SPENDING IN NEW YORK,
1977-78

Component of Per-Pupil Expenditures	*Level of Spending**		
	High	*Medium*	*Low*
Operating Expenditures	$2,863	$1,850	$1,325
Central District Admin	80 (3%)	42 (2%)	48 (3%)
Central District Services	329 (11%)	240 (13%)	156 (11%)
Instruction	1,822 (63%)	1,107 (59%)	800 (58%)
Employee Benefits	559 (19%)	373 (20%)	271 (20%)
Transportation	114 (4%)	105 (6%)	104 (8%)
Instructional Expenditures	$1,822	$1,102	$ 800
Curriculum Development & Supervision	175 (10%)	116 (10%)	55 (7%)
Teacher Salaries	1,303 (72%)	807 (73%)	619 (77%)
Non Instructional Salaries	28 (2%)	21 (2%)	9 (1%)
Books, Materials & Equipment	58 (3%)	41 (4%)	36 (5%)
Pupil Services	138 (8%)	71 (6%)	47 (6%)
Special Needs Students	$ 220	$ 219	$ 195
Teachers			
Pupil/Classroom Teachers	17.2	18.9	20.4
Median Teacher Salary	$22,037	$16,654	$12,716
Percent with only a B.A.	9.1	20.2	33.4
Percent with M.A. & 30 points or a Doctorate	35.9	15.3	6.0
Percent with more than 10 years experience	68.2	53.8	43.6

*High is top-spending decile; middle is decile 6; low is lowest spending decile.

Source: Odden, Palaich, and Augenblick (1979).

year; the numbers include state and local revenues only. First, instructional expenditures composed about 60 percent of state/local operating expenditures per pupil, quite close to the national average. Second, instructional expenditures per pupil as a percentage of total operating costs *increased* with spending levels, from 58 percent for the bottom decile, to 59 percent in the middle, to 63 percent for the top spending decile. This latter pattern was different from the Pennsylvania results discussed below, as well as different from later New York studies in the 1990s, also discussed below.

Employee benefit expenditures, often called fixed costs, consumed about 20 percent of expenditures across all spending levels, higher than the national figures. Expenditures for central-office administration and services also composed about an equal percentage of expenditures across all spending levels. Transportation, on the other hand, constituted a declining percentage of the budget as spending rose.

Spending for special-student needs, such as for compensatory and bilingual education, totaled about $200 per pupil for all three spending levels. Since the groups differed substantially in overall operating expenditures per pupil, this finding shows that spending for special-needs students constituted a much higher percentage of operating expenditures in low as compared to middle- or high-spending districts. This finding underscores the importance of a strong and fair state role in supporting services for special-needs students.

Although the percentage spent on instruction increased from just 58 to 63 percent, the dollar amount of the increase was larger, rising from $800 per pupil in the low-spending decile, to $1,107 in the middle and to $1,822 at the high-spending decile. These differences produced different patterns in expenditures for teachers. Low-spending districts spent 77 percent on teacher salaries, compared with only 72 percent in the high-spending districts. Nevertheless, the high-spending districts spent more than twice the per-pupil amount on teachers — $1,303 to $619. These higher expenditures were reflected primarily in different salaries; the median salaries were almost twice as high in the high-spending districts compared to the low-spending districts. Pupil-teacher ratios differed only marginally in New York, ranging from 20.3 in the lowest spending districts to 17.2 in the higher spending districts. In general, pupil-teacher ratios were uniformly low. Thus, differences in spending on teachers were reflected primarily in differences in teacher salary levels.

Some of these expenditure patterns had changed by 1992. As shown by the data in table 3.9, the major difference was that the percentage spent on instruction decreased as overall expenditures increased in 1992, a pattern than was much more typical across the country in the 1970s and 1980s, and a pattern more typical today as well. The data show that the percentage spent on some other categories in the 1970s and 1980s also increased with overall expenditures. As per-pupil expenditures rose, the percentages spent on administration, pupil services, maintenance and operations, and debt service also rose. Since the absolute amount spent is the product of the percentage times the overall expenditure level, higher spending districts not only spent more dollars on instruction (largely teacher salaries and benefits) but also on all these other elements of the budget.

The expenditure patterns across spending levels for Pennsylvania in both 1983-85 (Hartman 1988a and 1988b) and 1991-92 (Hartman 1993) were similar to the latter patterns in New York. Instructional expenditures as a percentage of current expenditures *decreased* as current spending increased. Although a larger portion of additional teacher expenditures was spent on reducing pupil-teacher ratios than on increasing teacher salaries, higher spending districts nevertheless both paid their teachers more and provided them lower class sizes. In terms of other patterns, higher spending districts had teachers with slightly more education and experience (though the differences were not as dramatic as in New York) and had more support and administrative personnel.

These studies show that higher spending districts are able to purchase a different mix of educational services than lower spending districts. They hire more teachers, administrators, and support personnel, hire teachers with more advanced education and years of experience, pay them more (sometimes dramatically more),

Table 3.9

**NEW YORK EXPENDITURES
BY FUNCTION AND BY SPENDING LEVEL,
1991-92**

Function	Quintile 1	Quintile 2	Quintile 3	Quintile 4	Quintile 5	Total
Instruction	62.5	62.2	62.0	61.9	60.0	61.8
Instructional Support	5.2	5.3	5.1	4.7	5.4	5.1
Administrative District State	9.9	10.2	9.9	10.1	11.0	10.2
Pupil Services	2.9	3.2	3.3	3.4	4.2	3.5
Maintenance & Operation	9.0	9.2	8.8	9.4	10.2	9.3
Transportation	6.4	6.1	6.4	6.5	6.3	6.3
Food	3.5	3.3	3.1	2.5	1.8	2.7
Debt Service	0.6	0.7	1.4	1.3	1.1	1.1
Total Expenditures	$6,067	$6,627	$7,309			

Each quintile includes about one-fifth of all students.

Source: Monk, Roellke, and Brent (1996), Table 3A.

have lower class sizes, provide more pupil-support services, and provide a greater variety of instructionally related support services.

In analyzing data from a larger and nationally representative sample of districts, Picus (1993a and 1993b) and Picus and Fazal (1996) found that higher spending districts tend generally to spend the bulk of their extra funds on more staff, and only a small amount on higher salaries. Their research found that higher spending districts spent about 50 percent of each additional dollar on more teachers, and the other 50 percent on noninstructional services. Of the 50 percent spent on teachers, 40 percentage points were used to hire more teachers and only 10 percentage points were used to provide higher salaries. Barro (1992) found similar results with state-level data; the bulk of extra revenues was used to hire more staff rather than for higher salaries.

But the schools tend not to use the additional staff for the regular instructional program, as partially hinted by the New York and Pennsylvania information above. In a fascinating analysis of 1991-92 teacher resources by core subject areas in New York secondary schools (English, mathematics, science, social studies, and foreign language), Monk, Roellke, and Brent (1996) showed that staffing in core subjects changed very little across district spending levels.

Table 3.10 shows the remarkable stability of the number of teachers per 1,000 students by five subject areas. Yes, teacher resources spiked a bit in the highest spending quintile, but only modestly. The average spending between the highest and lowest deciles differed by almost 100 percent, but teacher resources for the core academic subjects differed by only 20 percent. Teacher resources varied by negligible amounts across the four lowest spending quintiles, though spending varied by thousands of dollars.

However, though not systematically providing more resources for core academics, higher spending districts did spend more on some subjects than lower spending districts in New York. Monk, Roellke, and Brent (1996) found that higher spending districts spent significantly more on mathematics, and somewhat more on language arts, science, and social studies. Across all spending levels, districts tended to spend the most per pupil on science and foreign language, the second most on music, and the least on health and physical education.

Although its data are not disaggregated by spending level, the National Center for Education Statistics (1997) found that elementary teachers spend about one-third of their day on reading, half that (one-sixth) on mathematics, and half that (one-twelfth) on each of science and social studies. Taking the 60 percent spent on instruction, that means that approximately 20 cents of the education dollar is spent on elementary reading (60 percent times 1/3), 10 cents on mathematics, and five cents each on science and

Table 3.10

INSTRUCTIONAL STAFF PER 1,000 PUPILS BY SUBJECT
AREA IN NEW YORK SECONDARY SCHOOLS (GRADES 7-12),
1991-92

Subject	Quintile 1	Quintile 2	Quintile 3	Quintile 4	Quintile 5
English	5.20	5.25	5.43	5.31	6.10
Mathematics	4.46	4.51	4.67	4.54	5.00
Science	3.86	3.98	4.01	4.18	4.95
Social Studies	4.04	4.05	4.06	4.09	4.65
Foreign Language	2.18	2.36	2.35	2.46	3.23

Quintiles refer to spending levels, with Quintile 1 the lowest and Quintile 5 the highest.
Source: Monk, Roellke, and Brent (1996), Table 7a.

social studies, or about 30 cents of the dollar on teaching core academic subjects in elementary school.

In short, districts spend about 60 percent of their budget on instruction, but the percentage is a bit higher for lower spending districts and a bit lower for higher spending districts. But across all spending levels, instructional resources focused on the regular education program (mathematics, science, language arts/reading/writing, history, and foreign language) might not change significantly. As spending rises, more of the dollar is spent on nonregular instructional services, that is, "supports" for the regular instructional program—specialist teachers in resource rooms, more pupil support, and so forth.

The end result is that less than 50 percent of the education budget is spent on regular instruction at both secondary and elementary levels. This pattern also characterizes how the education system uses "new" money, addressed next. Although the resource deployment patterns reflect good values—putting money behind the special needs of many students—the question is whether other service strategies, and thus resource-use strategies, could be more effective with all students. The productivity question, for both the average as well as the special-needs student, is whether these expenditure behaviors provide the most "value added."

District Uses of New Money

These cross-sectional findings fit with longitudinal trends showing that rising real dollars per pupil have been accompanied by declines in the pupil-staff ratio; the average pupil-staff ratio fell from a high of 25 in 1960 to about 13 in 1990 (NCES 1993, table 31). These small pupil-staff ratios are at odds, however, with the large, actual class sizes of 30 or more students in many districts. The resolution of this dilemma illuminates how dollars and teacher resources typically are used in schools.

Historically and largely today as well, schools reflect a bureaucratic form of organization. Jobs are defined narrowly—principals manage schools and teachers teach students often with a fairly set curriculum and presumed or prescribed teaching strategies. As schools face new issues—such as greater numbers of disabled, low-achieving, and limited-English-language students and students with more emotional and psychological problems—programs are created that provide money for schools to hire "specialist" staff to deal with the issues.

Teachers remain in the regular classroom, and "specialists" are hired to teach disabled, low-achieving, and limited-English-language students in settings outside the regular classrooms, or to counsel and help students with emotional/psychological needs. Earlier examples of this phenomenon were the specialists added to school staffs to teach vocational education, physical education, and even art and music. Growth by addition and specialization has characterized the education system for several decades (Odden and Massy 1993).

Indeed, recent studies have shown that the vast bulk of new dollars provided to schools over the past 30 years was not spent on staff for the core instructional program but on specialist teachers and other resources to provide services to special-needs students usually outside of the regular classroom (Lankford and Wyckoff 1995; Rothstein and Miles 1995). Unfortunately, many other studies have shown that these programs and services have produced modest if any long-lasting effects on student achievement (Allington and Johnston 1989; Odden 1991). These dollars represent laudable values; low-income, disabled, and English-language-learning students need extra services. The values that provide the extra dollars for these extra services should be retained, but the productivity of the expenditure of these dollars needs to rise.

As a result of the increase of specialist staff and programs, regular classroom teachers—the primary service providers—compose a declining portion of professional staff in schools. The National Commission on Teaching and America's Future (1996) found that regular classroom teachers as a proportion of all professional staff fell from 70 percent in 1950 to 52 percent in 1995, with 10 percent of the latter not engaged in classroom teaching. The fiscal implication is that a declining portion of the education dollar is being spent on the core activity in schools—teaching the regular instructional program. These findings reinforce the data discussed at the beginning of this chapter.

The findings of these more recent studies are similar to those of the few studies on this topic conducted in the 1970s (Alexander 1973; Barro and Carroll 1975). Generally, these studies found that districts tended to use more money to increase nonteaching aspects of the budget, and that those dollars used to increase teacher expenditures were primarily used to increase teacher-student ratios, with only a small portion used to raise average teacher salary levels.

Related research in the 1990s on the local use of new money from school finance reforms has found similar patterns of resource use. Poor districts get more money and use it for clear needs (facilities, social services, compensatory education), but little of the new money makes it to the regular-education program (Adams 1994; Firestone, Goertz, Nagle, and Smelkinson 1994; Picus 1994c).

These findings in the 1990s differ from those of Kirst (1977) on the use of school finance reform dollars in California in the 1970s. He analyzed how spending changed in K-12 districts in Los Angeles County that received a 15 percent increase in state aid from a 1972 California school finance reform in response to the *Serrano v. Priest* court suit. He found that salary increases were marginal, in the 5-7 percent range. The bulk of new funds were used to hire additional instructional personnel, with some funds used to reduce class size, some to add periods to the school day, and some to hire specialists. Although the specific roles of the new staff varied across districts, all exhibited a pattern of hiring more professional personnel rather than hiking salaries or salary schedules.

In an econometric analysis of local district response to increased funds from a major 1980s education reform, Picus (1988) found that districts increased instructional expenditures more in response to fiscal incentives to increase the length of the school day and year than in response to increases in unrestricted general aid revenue.* In analyzing the data over multiple time periods, Picus also found that these boosts in instructional expenditure dissipated when California "rolled" the incentive funds into the district's general-aid grant.

The end result is a system in which when money rises, services expand outside the regular classroom, but results in terms of student achievement stay flat or improve by only small amounts.

Resource-Use Patterns at the Site Level

We are beginning to know more about how the education dollar is being spent at the school-site level. The culprit for our lack of knowledge in the past has been, in part, the accounting system. For years, school districts tracked expenditures only by objects such as salaries, benefits, books and other instructional materials, supplies, rent or operations and maintenance, and other specific objects of expenditures. Then, in the 1970s accounting

---

*This finding is consistent with predictions derived from intergovernmental grant theory.

systems began to change to organize object expenditures into functional categories such as the following:

1. Administration, sometimes divided between site and central-office administration

2. Instruction, sometimes but usually not divided between direct classroom instruction and instructional support such as staff development and curriculum development

3. Operations and maintenance

4. Transportation

5. Fixed charges such as employee benefits (unfortunately, not linked to the different salary expenditures that induced the benefits charge)

6. Capital

7. Debt service

This grouping of expenditures represented a step forward.

In the 1980s, these changes were complemented by accounting programs that tracked expenditures by program—regular instruction, compensatory education, special education, and so forth. Both changes represented advances. But few states use these accounting codes to indicate expenditures by function and program at the school-site level, an issue discussed in the next section.

Expenditures by School and Classroom

Two major studies on expenditures by school and classroom form the current information base on how funds are used below the district level. Table 3.11 presents 1985-86 California expenditures on a *school* basis (Guthrie, Kirst, and Odden 1990). The numbers represent a statewide average for all schools, thus merging data for elementary, middle, and high schools, for which expenditure patterns undoubtedly differ. Nevertheless, it was one of the first studies that provided information on expenditures on a school level.

The table shows that 63 percent of all expenditures were spent directly on classroom services, which is close to the portion spent on instruction as reported by studies of state and district spending patterns noted in the preceding sections. Only 50 percent was

Table 3.11

CALIFORNIA EXPENDITURES PER SCHOOL, 1985-1986

Category	Expenditures per School	Percent of Total
Classroom Expenditures	$1,286,000	63
22 Classroom Teachers	914,000	45
2.5 Specialized Instructors	102,000	5
7.0 Instructional Aides	94,000	5
2.0 Pupil Personnel Support	84,000	4
Books, Supplies, Equipment	92,000	4
Other Site Expenditures	629,000	31
Operation, Maintenance & Transportation	395,000	19
Instructional Support	95,000	5
School Site Leadership	139,000	7
District/County Administration	120,000	5.5
State Department of Education	11,000	0.5
Total Operating Expenditures	$2,046,000	100
School Facilities/Capital	$133,000	

Source: Guthrie, Kirst , and Odden (1990).

spent on classroom and specialized teachers. How was the other 13 percent spent in the classroom? Instructional aides constituted one large portion, at 5 percent; pupil-personnel support such as guidance counselors constituted another 4 percent; and books, supplies, and equipment composed the remaining 4 percent. Thus, the data indicate that about two-thirds of expenditures were on direct classroom services.

What were the noninstructional elements that received the remaining one-third of expenditures? First, about 31 percent was spent on other site-related items—site administration, site instructional support including curriculum support and staff development, and operations, maintenance, and transportation. Only 6 percent was spent on district, county, and state administration. Thus, 37 percent of California 1986-87 *school-site* expenditures were spent on nonclassroom activities. Hayward (1988) shows that for many of these expenditure items, the amount spent per item (such as per meal served, per student transported, per square foot of physical plant, and so forth) was below norms in the private sector, suggesting that school system expenditures were not profligate.

These figures begin to take the mystery out of how educational dollars are spent. Although only 50 percent of each dollar was spent on teachers, the other 50 percent was not simply wasted. While the efficiency of expenditures in all categories can be examined, the fact is that all categories of expenditures are needed. Students must be transported to school. Schools must be operated, heated or cooled, and maintained. Some central administration is necessary, and 6 percent is not a large figure. Books, materials, supplies, and instructional support services are needed.

In short, nonteacher expenditures are not lost in an alleged "administrative blob," though these other expenditures are noninstructional. Although a dramatically restructured school could have different spending patterns and produce more student learning, current spending patterns are not irrational. The route to improving school productivity is not in attacking administrative costs, though such costs are probably too high in many districts. Rather, it is determining what works to boost student learning and making sure dollars support those strategies.

National data on *classroom* expenditures generally confirm these California subdistrict school expenditure patterns. Table 3.12 shows nationwide classroom expenditures for 1984-85 (Fox 1987). These numbers likewise aggregate elementary, middle, and high schools to represent an average classroom. The table shows that "other expenditures," including transportation, operation and maintenance, food services, and fixed charges, constituted about one-third (33.2 percent) of total expenditures. Nonsite administration constituted another 7.2 percent.

Table 3.12

NATIONWIDE EXPENDITURES PER CLASSROOM, 1984-85

Item of Expenditure	*Amount (Percent of Total)*
Total	$78,422
Nonsite Administration	5,646 (7.2)
District & State Admin.	3,058 (3.9)
Clerks (District & Site)	2,588 (3.3)
Site Administration	2,353 (3.0)
Principals	1,647 (2.1)
Assistant Principals	706 (0.9)
Instruction	43,801 (55.6)
Teachers	23,546 (30.0)
Curriculum Specialists & Other Classroom Teachers	8,336 (10.4)
Other Professional Staff	1,490 (1.9)
Teacher Aids	1,804 (2.3)
Library Media Specialists	549 (0.7)
Guidance & Counseling	1,176 (1.5)
Instructional Materials	6,430 (8.2)
Pupil Support Services, Attendance, Health	470 (0.6)
Other Non-Administration & Instruction	26,036 (33.2)
Maintenance	8,783 (11.2)
Transportation	3,451 (4.4)
Food Service	3,137 (4.0)
Fixed Charges (Insurance, benefits, etc.)	10,665 (13.6)

Source: Fox (1987).

Instruction and site administration composed 58.6 percent of total expenditures, with classroom teachers and other specialist teachers constituting 40.4 percent of total expenditures. Indeed, these national data show that the percentages of expenditures on teachers nationwide were lower than in California, and that the percentages spent on instruction and site administration were somewhat below that spent in California.

Average Expenditures by School Level

Drawing upon the Schools and Staffing Survey for 1993-94, table 3.13 shows the staffing in a national average elementary, middle, and high school. Although the data do not show non-professional staff expenditures, the data provide additional insights into how the education dollar is spent. At the elementary level, the numbers show that the school would need 20 teachers to provide regular class sizes of 25 students. Since the school on average has 27 teachers, that means it has seven additional teachers probably used for such purposes as music, art, and physical education to provide regular teachers "planning and preparation" time, as well as specialist teachers for special-needs programs. These schools also have a librarian and a half-time media aide, and 2.5 counselors and other pupil-support personnel. The average elementary school also has 6.0 instructional aides.

In sum, the national average elementary school has several professional resources above the "core" of one teacher for every 25 students. Using national average figures for salaries and benefits (about $50,000 a position), the average elementary school spends $640,000 beyond "core" resources.

Interestingly, for each grouping of 500 students, middle schools and high schools have approximately the same level of additional funds. For each level of school, these staffing resources are in addition to resources for other items such as instructional materials, books, and professional development.

The data confirm that schools on average had a substantial level of resources, over and above what is required to provide a regular class size of 25. Again, the productivity question focuses

Table 3.13

SCHOOL STAFFING RESOURCES IN NATIONAL AVERAGE ELEMENTARY, MIDDLE, AND HIGH SCHOOLS

Ingredient	Elementary School Grades K-5*	Middle School Grades 6-8**	High School Grades 9-12***
Average Enrollment	500	1000	1500
1. Principal	1.0	1.0	1.0
2. Assistant Principals	0.0	2.0	3.0
3. Teachers	27.0	57.5	85.5
4. Librarians and Media	1.5	2.0	3.0
5. Media Aides			
6. Counselors & Psychologists	2.5	4.0	6.0
7. Teacher Aides	6.0	5.0	6.0
8. Total Staff Resources****	$1,690,000	$3,400,000	$5,015,000
9. Total CORE Resources	1 Principal; 20 teachers $1,050,000	1 Principal; 40 teachers $2,050,000	1 Principal; 60 teachers $3,050,000
10. Total Above CORE (Line 8 minus Line 9) (per 500 students)	$640,000 ($640,000)	$1,350,000 ($675,000)	$1,965,000 ($655,000)

    * Enrollments from 400 to 600 students.
    ** Enrollments from 900 to 1,100 students.
    *** Enrollments from 1,400 to 1,600 students.
    ****Average professional staff cost at $50,000; average teacher aide cost at $15,000.
Source: Staffing data from analysis of Schools and Staffing Survey, 1993-94.

on productive use of these resources. It is a "given" that special needs of students must be met, and some portion of the additional resources must be devoted to these needs. But the overall question is which pattern of resource use will provide the most benefit for both the average student and the student with special needs.

School finance experts would like to know more about resource allocation and use at the site level. We would like both detailed staffing data and expenditure data by function and program. As chapter 5 explains, a few states have moved on this agenda, and others are moving or thinking of moving on this agenda.

CHAPTER 4

Class-Size Reduction: Effects and Relative Costs

$\mathbf{P}$erhaps the hottest state educational policy initiative in the nation today is the move to reduce class size, particularly in the primary (K-3) grades. In recent years, a number of states have passed legislation either mandating smaller classes in elementary grades or establishing incentive programs to finance smaller classes.

Few public policy proposals are more popular than class-size reduction. In March 1997, a *Wall Street Journal* poll found that 70 percent of adults believed reducing class size would lead to big improvements for public schools. A 1997 *Education Week* survey found that 83 percent of teachers and 60 percent of principals believed classes should not exceed 17 students (Bell 1998). Parents say their children are happier and learn more in smaller classes. Teachers report they have fewer discipline problems, are able to give students more individual help, and can cover material faster.

Many states have enacted class-size-reduction measures in recent years. Perhaps best known is California's effort to reduce the size of all K-3 classrooms to no more than 20 students. Tennessee has had a program in place since 1990 to reduce class size, while Texas mandates that all K-4 classrooms in a school average no more than 22 students. Most states that implement class-size reduction seem to set average K-3 class size at around 20 students. Nevada has the lowest mandated size, requiring no more than 15 students per class. Washington has used its basic aid school finance distribution formula to provide additional funding to increase the number of certificated instructional staff members per 1,000 students on a number of occasions.

The continued and growing popularity of this reform was evident in 1998 when President Clinton called for hiring 100,000 new teachers to reduce class size to an average of 18 students in grades 1-3. He also proposed a construction tax to help build and modernize schools to help pay for the estimated $12 billion it would cost to provide enough classrooms.

Dramatic class-size reduction is expensive. California's program provides an additional $800 per student for children in K-3 classrooms with 20 or fewer students. It also provided funds for school and classroom construction. To reduce the class size from an average of approximately 29 to 20 or fewer students, the first-year costs of the program were some $1.1 billion. By the end of the program's fourth year (1999-00), the state will have spent more than $6 billion on class-size reduction. This observation is in line with general estimates offered by Brewer, Krop, Gill, and Reichardt (1999).

Other states have made similar investments. Tennessee spent about $600 million between 1991 and 1996 to implement its program. In Philadelphia, Superintendent David Hornbeck has unveiled plans to reduce class size in kindergarten through third grade from an average of 27 students to 20 students by the year 2002. He estimates that the program will require 1,000 new teachers at a cost of $50 million a year, as well as 35 new schools at a construction cost of $470 million. Philadelphia school district's annual budget is approximately $1.2 billion. Washington estimates that the cost of its class-size-reduction incentives has been between $250 and $300 million.

Class-size-reduction efforts become progressively more expensive as class size decreases. For example, a hypothetical district with 10,000 students would need to add about 22 teachers (and classroom space) to move from 22 to 21 students per teacher (a 4.5 percent reduction). However, it would take about 42 more teachers to move from 16 to 15 students per teacher (a 6.3 percent reduction). Figure 4.1 shows the number of additional teachers needed to reduce class size to progressively lower levels.

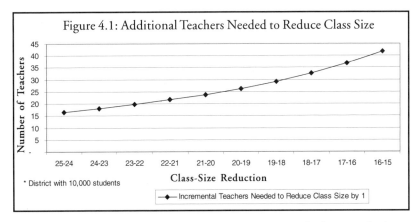

Figure 4.1: Additional Teachers Needed to Reduce Class Size

Aside from new teachers, new spaces are needed to teach these students. Brewer and colleagues (1999) estimated that, to reach a required class size of 20 students, at the current rate we would need 41,574 new classroom spaces. That number increases as class-size limits decrease. If class sizes were set at 15 as they were in Nevada and the Tennessee Star Project, we would need an estimated 221,612 new classrooms to teach these students in reduced classes. This recent estimate reaffirms the billion-dollar price tag that accompanies class-size reduction.

Although current research supports the notion that smaller class size can lead to improved student performance, that view is not universally held among researchers. More important, research shows that alternative reforms may be considerably more cost-effective in improving student performance. In particular, many have argued that investments in additional teacher training and professional development will lead to even greater gains in student performance for each dollar spent. It is important to understand both the policy and research context of the class-size-reduction issue.

The next section establishes the policy context for the discussion of class-size reduction. The second section briefly reviews the research literature on the effectiveness of smaller classes on student performance. In the third section, alternative policy options are discussed and compared with class-size-reduction programs.

Class-Size Reduction:
The Policy Context

National Trends

Reducing class size to improve education is not a new idea. Data from the federal government show that the average pupil-teacher ratio in the United States has declined dramatically in the last 40 years (NCES 1997).

Figure 4.2 shows that the pupil-teacher ratio in the United States has declined from nearly 27:1 in 1955 to approximately 17:1 in 1997. Some of this reduction can be accounted for by the increased availability of special programs (Title I and special

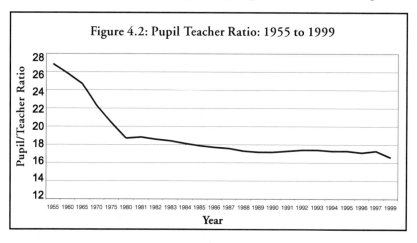

Figure 4.2: Pupil Teacher Ratio: 1955 to 1999

education) for poor and mentally and physically challenged children; these programs utilize very small classes or rely on "pull-out" programs that require a teacher to work with children individually or in small groups. Nevertheless, the data displayed in figure 4.2 represent real declines in the average number of children in most classrooms across the United States.

Nationally, as per-pupil spending has increased, pupil-teacher ratios have declined. Figure 4.3 shows this trend graphically for the years 1955 through 1997. The vertical axis on the left side of figure 4.3 represents the pupil-teacher ratio, while the vertical axis on the right side represents per-pupil spending. The figure

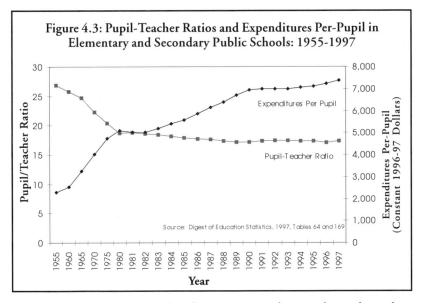

Figure 4.3: Pupil-Teacher Ratios and Expenditures Per-Pupil in Elementary and Secondary Public Schools: 1955-1997

Source: Digest of Education Statistics, 1997, Tables 64 and 169

shows an inverse relationship between spending and pupil-teacher ratios.

Research by Barro (1992) found that, on average, when a school district received an additional dollar of revenue, half of that dollar was spent on teachers. Of those 50 cents, 40 cents were spent on reducing class size and 10 cents on increasing salaries. Barro's findings help confirm the apparent priority educators place on smaller classes, and their willingness to trade increases in salary for smaller classes.

Why Is There Such Strong Policy Interest in Smaller Class Size?

As noted in the opening section of this chapter, the cost of implementing smaller class size is high. Brewer and others (1999) go on to note that policy goals and foundation-level policy requirements play a major role in dictating the cost of implementing and maintaining smaller class sizes. Depending on the baseline policy option (size of class) adhered to, the cost of class-size reduction could range anywhere from $2 billion to $11 billion per year, say Brewer and colleagues. They estimated the cost of implementing class sizes at varying levels: 20 students as is the case in

California, 18 as proposed by the federal program, and 15 as carried out in Tennessee's project STAR.

Further, Brewer and others' framework assumed that various policy issues—grade level, eligibility, phase-in period, measurement level, and flexibility—significantly influence the cost of implementing CSR. Also, Brewer and others show that the cost of maintaining smaller class size rises yearly, from total operational costs of $5.049 billion dollars and $448 per pupil in operational cost in the 1998-99 school year to an estimated $6.028 billion and $562 per pupil in operating cost in 2007-2008.

Despite these current and future high costs, legislative efforts to reduce class size are common. Today in Washington, districts generate 3 more certificated instructional staff positions per 1,000 students in grades K-3 than they do for grades 4-12. Moreover, additional incentives—not part of a district's basic aid—allow that staffing ratio to be as much as 8.3 certificated instructional staff members per 1,000 students higher in grades K-3. The K-3 pupil-teacher ratio can therefore be as low as 18.42, or some 3.32 pupils per teacher fewer than the pupil-teacher ratio of 21.74 generated in grades 4-12, where the formula provides 46 certificated instructional staff members per 1,000 pupils.

One of the first states to enact CSR was Texas, which began mandating limited class sizes with the educational reforms of 1984. Today, K-4 programs must average no more than 22 students per classroom. Of the 19 states that have some form of class-size reduction, 10 rely on incentives to encourage school districts to reduce class size, whereas 8 use mandates (Education Commission of the States 1998). Washington is unique in that it relies on both a mandate and an incentive if districts spend the funds on certificated instructional staff members who work with students in grades K-3.

The focus of state programs is almost entirely on the primary grades, generally K-3. North Carolina's program is aimed at grades K-2, while Oklahoma's program focuses on grades K-6, and the program in Texas on grades K-4. In Utah, grades K-2 are the primary focus, and funds can be devoted to reducing class size in grades 3 and 4 only if K-2 classes already are all reduced to 18 or lower.

Washington's program differs to some extent from the others in that the law does not require classes of 18 or 20 or some other number, only that the funds be spent on staff members who work with children in grades K-3. Theoretically this allows for alternative staffing structures as determined by schools and their respective districts.

There is no question that class-size reductions are an important educational policy issue. They can also be very expensive, as the data above suggest. The general belief of most educators and policymakers is that smaller classes are effective in improving student performance. However, it is difficult to ascertain the "right" class size and to determine whether the positive effects of being in a small class in grades K-3 stay with students into later grades. Essentially, the investment is hardly worthwhile if student outcomes do not improve over the long run. The next section considers the research on class size, particularly its impact on student achievement.

Reducing Class Size: A Brief Synthesis of the Literature

Today, it is hard to find anyone not in favor of reducing class size. Even those who are not convinced there is a strong research base to show that smaller classes lead to improved student performance are willing to concede that smaller classes can lead to more individualized instruction, higher morale among teachers, and more opportunities for teachers to implement instructional programs that research shows work well. Among those who are convinced that smaller classes lead to better student performance, there is only limited consensus on what the "ideal" class size might be. By looking at those studies that appear to be the most methodologically sound, this section attempts to provide answers to three questions:

- Does class-size reduction improve student learning?
- What is the "ideal" class size?
- Do gains in primary grades continue in the later grades?

The section begins by describing the early meta-analyses on class size and then discusses recent studies that have attempted to resolve some of the methodological issues identified with earlier studies.

Research Results

Researchers have struggled with ways to correct for these limitations. While new and more sophisticated statistical techniques and higher quality data sets at the district, state, and federal levels have improved the quality of production-functions analyses, the analysis will never be perfect. The following subsections describe the results of this research to date.

The Early Meta-Analyses

Meta-analysis (Glass, McGaw, and Smith 1981) is a technique for looking at a wide variety of studies on a specific topic and determining if the results of those studies support a conclusion about that topic. The first step is to identify high-quality studies on the subject. This is done by searching for all the documents dealing with the topic and establishing decision rules about whether to include each study in the meta-analysis. These decision rules usually pertain to the quality of the study (that is, published in a refereed journal or high-quality book) and the relevance of the actual analysis to the topic of the meta-analysis.

Once studies to be included in the meta-analysis have been identified, researchers need to compare the findings. This is difficult since studies use different data sets, have different sample sizes, and analyze different variables. To compare studies, the results are standardized and the outcomes compared in terms of these standardized values.*

Glass and Smith (1979) conducted an early and comprehensive meta-analysis of the class-size literature. They identified more

---

* The results are standardized or normalized so that each has a mean of zero and a standard deviation of one. Then, the effects of each variable on the outcome measure can be expressed in terms of standard deviations and thus compared. For example, an overall impact of half a standard deviation means that student performance would rise from the average or 50th percentile to the 69th percentile, and an impact of one standard deviation would mean average performance would rise all the way to the 83rd percentile.

than 300 studies on the topic going back as far as 1895. Of those 300, 77 met their decision rules for inclusion in the meta-analysis. They calculated a total of 725 effects from the 77 studies. Based on their analysis of those studies, Glass and Smith concluded:

- There is a clear and strong relationship between class size and student achievement. Sixty percent of the 725 effects showed higher achievement in smaller classes.
- Students learned more in small classes.
- Class size needed to be reduced to fewer than 20 students, preferably to 15, if strong impacts on student learning were to be found.

These are strong and important conclusions, and many have used them to support calls for reducing class size to fewer than 20. However, not everyone in the research community found this work to be convincing. Slavin (1984) criticized meta-analysis, arguing that the technique gives equal weight to all study findings, regardless of the quality of the study design. He argued that only 14 of the 77 studies in the Glass and Smith meta-analysis were methodologically sound. He also criticized meta-analysis generally, suggesting that the technique combines studies that are on different topics while claiming to address the same topic. For example, one of the methodologically sound studies with large effects in the Glass and Smith sample had to do with learning how to play tennis.

When Slavin (1989) reanalyzed the methodologically sound studies from the Glass and Smith work, he pointed out that there were relatively few studies with fewer than 20 students in a class, and that there were no classes with between 4 and 14 students. He argued that the Glass and Smith findings were thus based on statistical interpolations of the findings in the 14 sound studies. He also concluded that the effects of reduced class size on student achievement were considerably smaller than Glass and Smith had determined.

Using these data from earlier meta-analyses, Odden (1990) suggested that the research supports "dramatic—and only dramatic—class size reductions." While he did not necessarily specify what class size should be, Odden argued that reducing class size from 28 to 26, or from 24 to 22, would not be effective. He argued that class size needed to be reduced substantially more—to something like 15 to 17 students per class. This line of reasoning has major implications for policymakers interested in reducing class size. States with large class sizes will need to spend substantial sums of money to make those "dramatic" reductions if the policy is to succeed.

Recent Studies

In recent years a number of studies have analyzed the impact of class size on student learning. In general, they show that smaller class size leads to greater gains in student test scores. One exception to this is the work of Eric Hanushek, who argues that to date we have not found a systematic relationship between resources and student outcomes. Hanushek (1989) reviewed 152 studies that used the pupil-teacher ratio as an independent variable in estimating the impact of spending and resources on student outcomes. Hanushek found only 27 studies with statistically significant findings, and only 14 of those found that reducing the number of pupils per teacher was positively correlated to student outcomes, whereas 13 found the opposite. Among the other 125, Hanushek found 34 with a positive effect, 46 with a negative effect, and 45 with an undetermined effect.

More recently, Hedges, Laine, and Greenwald (1994) and Greenwald, Hedges, and Laine (1996a), after reviewing the same studies, came to the opposite conclusion. Relying on newer and more sophisticated statistical techniques, they argued that smaller classes did matter. Their analysis found substantial gains in student performance when more money was spent on education, and smaller class size was related to performance gains as well.

Others have reached that conclusion as well. Ferguson (1991) analyzed the effect of class size and teacher preparation on student achievement in Texas, concluding that in elementary grades lower pupil-teacher ratios contributed to increases in student achievement. In a recent study in Alabama, Ferguson and Ladd (1996) attempted to address some of the weaknesses of earlier studies in this area. They used larger samples of students, employed better model specification, and had access to better data than in the past. They concluded that teacher test scores, teacher education, and class size "appear to affect student learning" (Ferguson and Ladd 1996). They also attempted to ascertain the threshold below which further reductions in class size would no longer lead to systematic achievement gains for students. They believe that if such a threshold exists, it is in the range of 23 to 25 students per teacher. This number seems somewhat high compared to other results, but could be a result of the relatively low per-pupil spending in Alabama and the generally larger class size in that state during their study. More important, Ferguson and Ladd sought to measure actual class size, rather than the district's or school's pupil-teacher ratio. Consequently, their work may reflect a more accurate picture of the number of students in a classroom at any time.

One of the problems with this line of research has been the lack of a true experimental design. In fact, only one study with such a design has been undertaken. The Tennessee Student-Teacher Achievement Ratio project (STAR) relied on an experiment in which children were randomly assigned to classes with low pupil-teacher ratios and high pupil-teacher ratios. The study design placed students into one of three groups: an experimental group where the average class size was 15.1 students and two control groups (a regular-size class with an average of 22.4 students and a regular-size class with a teacher's aide and an average class size of 22.8 students).

Under the study plan, each student was to stay in the original class-size assignment until the third grade. Following third grade, the experiment was concluded and all students assigned to regular-size classrooms. Standardized tests were given each school year to measure student achievement. While there are some methodological and data problems in any study of this magnitude, two respected researchers have argued that the Tennessee STAR project is the best-designed experimental study on this topic to date (Mosteller 1995, Kruger 1998). Kruger (1998) summarized the major findings of the Tennessee STAR project as follows:

- At the end of the first year of the study, the performance of students in the experimental classes exceeded that of the students in the two control groups by five to eight percentile points.

- For students who started the program in kindergarten, the relative advantage for students assigned to small classes grew between kindergarten and first grade, but beyond that the difference is relatively small.

- For students who entered in the first or second grade, the advantage of being in a small class tended to grow in subsequent grades.

- There is little difference in the performance of students in the regular-size classrooms compared to the performance of students in regular-size classrooms with teacher aides.

- Minority students and students who qualify for free and reduced-price lunches tended to receive a larger benefit from being assigned to small classes.

- Students who were in small classes have shown lasting achievement gains through the seventh grade.

A number of important policy issues are highlighted by the findings from Tennessee's STAR project. First, the results of the evaluation suggest that smaller classes do lead to improved student performance, and that those performance gains are maintained at least through the seventh grade. Recently, Nye, Hedges, and Konstantopoulos, in a five-year followup study, wrote that although some students "dropped out," they dropped out having attained a higher level of achievement than their peers in larger classes. Moreover, the results suggest that alternative models that rely on the use of teacher aides to reduce the "effective class size" may be ineffective.

The research also suggests that simply reducing class size without changing how teachers of smaller classes deliver instruction is unlikely to improve student performance. It is important that teachers take advantage of the smaller classes to offer material in new and challenging ways identified through research. Absent that effort and the training needed to accompany such a change, expenditures for class-size reduction may be relatively ineffective.

Alternatives to Class-Size Reduction

The research reviewed above shows that reducing class size can, and probably does, lead to improved student performance. It is, however, a very expensive option: In addition to hiring more teachers, schools need additional classroom space. Before embarking on a substantial CSR program, policymakers may want to consider whether more cost-effective alternatives exist. Current research suggests that such alternatives are available and should be considered, either instead of—or in addition to—class-size reduction. One range of options deals with teacher knowledge and skills, while others relate to the structure of the education program offered at individual schools. Each is discussed below.

Teacher Knowledge and Skills

Reducing class size gives students greater access to teacher resources. There is evidence this improved access will help students learn. However, what the teacher knows and is able to do is at least as important in helping students learn.

Darling-Hammond (1998) argues that "teacher expertise is one of the most important factors in determining student achievement." She quotes Greenwald, Hedges, and Laine's work, which demonstrated the relative impact of spending $500 more per pupil on increased teacher education, increased teacher experience, and increased teacher salaries. All three of these appear to have a greater impact on student test scores than does lowering the pupil-teacher ratio. Figure 4.4 shows the differences graphically. For an expenditure of $500, the greatest gains in student test scores (measured in standard deviation units from a range of tests in 60 studies) were achieved through increasing teacher education. Lowering the "pupil-teacher ratio was the least cost effective of the four methods. Increasing teacher salaries and experience fell between lower pupil-teacher ratios and teacher education in terms of cost effectiveness."

Ferguson (1991) found that the effects of teacher expertise in Texas were so great that after controlling for socioeconomic status, disparities in achievement between black and white students were virtually entirely explained by differences in teacher qualifi-

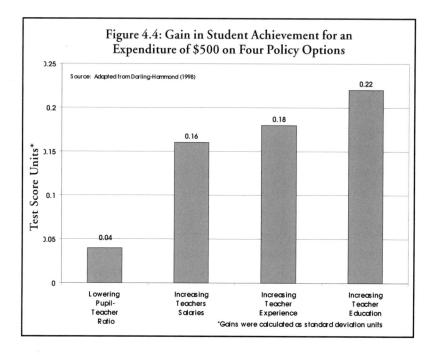

Figure 4.4: Gain in Student Achievement for an Expenditure of $500 on Four Policy Options

cations. He found that teacher qualifications explained 43 percent of the variation among the factors affecting math score test gains, whereas small classes and schools only accounted for 8 percent of the gain. Home and family factors were identified as explaining the remaining 49 percent of the variance.

Darling-Hammond (1998) summarizes these findings by stating that "teachers who know a lot about teaching and learning and who work in settings that allow them to know their students well are the critical elements of successful learning." Smaller classes are clearly desirable in her view, but given limited funds to invest, her work suggests policymakers should at least take a close look at improving access to high-quality professional development first.

Professional development is frequently poorly funded in school districts and often the first item to be cut when finances become tight. Darling-Hammond's research suggests this may be a mistake, and, in fact, more resources should be put into professional development. Even if class size is reduced, professional development still may be essential to help teachers maximize their skills and capitalize on the benefits of having a reduced number of children for whom they are responsible. Certainly investments in professional development would be complementary to class-size-reduction programs.

Reducing class size and providing greater training opportunities for teachers are not the only options available for improving student learning. There are many things school-board members and site leaders themselves can do to restructure their schools for improved learning. Several of these are briefly discussed below.

Reorganizing Schools

Many of today's educational reforms are restructuring how educational resources are used. A number of the reform designs supported by the New American Schools (NAS), for example, rely on using teaching resources differently, rather than purchasing more. While seven designs supported by NAS require some investment on the part of a school or school district, most are less expensive than dramatic reductions in class size or pupil-teacher ratios.* Most also come with substantial teacher-training components.

Odden and Busch (1998) found substantial gains in student performance, often as high as one-third of a standard deviation, at NAS design schools. These schools reach these performance levels with relatively little additional expenditures, generally averaging around $50,000 to $250,000 a year for a school of 500 students (an extra $100 to $500 per pupil each year). Odden and Busch argue that any school can reorganize itself into one of the NAS designs by looking closely at its current allocation of teachers and aides and reassigning them as needed to meet the design specifications. In many instances this calls for eliminating aides in favor of more teachers. Given the results of the Tennessee STAR

---

* The seven school designs supported by the New American Schools include the Modern Red Schoolhouse; Expeditionary Learning-Outward Bound; National Alliance; Audrey Cohen College; Co-NECT; ATLAS; and Roots and Wings (New American Schools 1996; Stringfield, Ross, and Smith 1996). An eighth design, Urban Learning Center Schools, was not part of the Odden and Busch analysis.

project reported above, spending for teacher aides may not be productive anyway.

In a more recent study of five schools, Odden and Archibald (2000) found that all of them were able to reorganize and reallocate resources to improve student achievement with relatively little additional money. The schools appear to have succeeded by redirecting many of their categorical funds away from programs they viewed as ineffective and toward programs viewed as better meeting the needs of each school's children.

Another option schools can consider is restructuring the use of time. The National Commission on Time and Learning (1994) reported on a number of successful schools and school districts that had improved student performance through different ways of organizing the school day to give students more access to, and time with, teachers. Models that provide more access to learning resources, particularly teachers, may also be substantially more cost-effective than class-size reduction.

Conclusion

Class-size reduction is one of the most popular—and most expensive—educational reforms today. At least 19 states have enacted mandatory or voluntary policies aimed at reducing class size in the primary grades, and one (California) has even created an incentive to reduce the number of students in ninth-grade English and math classes.

State policymakers face this question: Should substantial investments in smaller classes be made? The research shows that such investments will lead to improved student outcomes. However, the research also indicates that attention to teacher training and expertise may have a bigger payoff per dollar spent. Moreover, as California's experience shows, states that jump into a major CSR program quickly may find they have a shortage of qualified teachers. Given the importance of high-quality teaching to student learning, investment in the quality of the teaching force first might be a better way to maximize the potential of the dollars that are used to reduce class size.

In short, few appear to oppose class-size reduction. However, reducing class size is only one of the things states and school districts can do to ensure that the substantial investment made in teachers and classrooms pays off to the maximum extent possible. Virtually all the policy options revolve around ensuring that the state has the highest quality teaching force possible.

CHAPTER 5

The Collection and Use of School-Level Data

In recent years, a number of states have begun to collect school-level data in an effort to learn more about the financial operation of schools and to hold schools and school districts more accountable for student performance. Florida has been collecting these data for over 20 years, and other states have entered the fray more recently. Ohio and Texas currently have school-level databases, while South Carolina is in the process of establishing school-level data (Tetreault 1998). Also, Oregon is in the process of developing a comprehensive, school-level fiscal system for its schools.

This chapter provides a general overview of the issues surrounding the collection of school-level data from schools and school districts. In addition to informing readers about the uses and benefits of school-level data, the chapter discusses in general terms the problems some states have had in implementing such collection efforts.

The first section summarizes current thinking about the benefits of school-level data-collection efforts, while the second offers a summary of the complexities and issues that need to be resolved in the design of a school-level data-collection system. The third section summarizes the research that has been undertaken to date using school-level data from states where such data exist.

The original version of this chapter was prepared as a technical report to the Washington Joint Legislative Audit and Review Committee.

Why Collect School-Level Data?

Recent research from the private sector suggests that devolving more responsibility to the unit of production often results in more efficient and profitable production (Lawler 1986). More information about the fiscal status of individual schools could help answer questions about the impact additional revenues might have on student performance. The ability to analyze inputs and outputs of the educational system closer to the "unit of production"—the school building rather than the district—is an attractive reason for considering school-level data collections. Similarly, school-level analyses will help focus attention on the outputs or student outcomes of each school individually and on the relationship between inputs and outputs or outcomes.

The collection of school-level data is much more than the simple collection of data on school-level revenues and expenditures. In addition to basic fiscal data, school-level data systems need information about school (and district) staff and students. Staffing databases—which are more frequently available at the school-level than are fiscal databases—need to include information about both certificated and classified staff. At a minimum, it seems information would be needed about type of assignments, salary level, qualifications and education, and the full-time equivalent percentage of time an individual works. Similarly, student databases would need to provide accurate counts of enrollments, student counts for state attendance purposes (which is typically different from enrollment), course enrollments, information about the students' demographic and socioeconomic status, and assessment data. Fortunately, today the technology exits for collecting and using school-level data.

Collecting all these data at the school level is highly labor intensive and consequently very expensive. Prior to undertaking an effort of this magnitude and expense, the limitations of only collecting data at the district level should be considered.

The Limitations of District-Level Data

School finance has traditionally focused on the school district. Most school funding formulas distribute money to districts.

To date, school finance equity efforts have focused on district-level equity. Realizing the limits of district-level data, the Finance Center of the Consortium for Policy Research in Education (CPRE)* sought to develop a better understanding of how educational resources are allocated and used. Using a multilevel approach, research teams analyzed large federal databases including the Bureau of the Census reports on government spending and the School and Staffing Survey (Picus 1993a and 1993b). They also attempted to analyze finance and staff data collected by individual states that had—or claimed to have—school-level data capability (Hertert 1996; Nakib 1996; Monk, Roellke, and Brent 1996; Odden, Monk, Nakib, and Picus 1995). Finally, teams of researchers conducted multiyear case studies in four school districts in each of three states (Firestone, Goertz, Nagle, and Smelkinson 1994; Adams 1994; Picus 1994a).

CPRE researchers were surprised to find that school districts look more alike than different. On average, school districts spend about 60 percent of their funds on instruction and the remaining 40 percent on all other educational services including administration, maintenance and operations, instructional support, transportation, food services, and others. This pattern is unrelated to location or level of spending. For example, even though New Jersey spends roughly twice as much per pupil as California, the same 60/40 ratio exists. This does not mean that things are the same in those two states. The higher spending level in New Jersey allows school districts to offer smaller classes and pay teachers more compared to California. Moreover, there is a much richer mix of support services available to schools and students in New

---

*CPRE, the Consortium for Policy Research in Education, is a consortium of six universities that conduct research on educational policy. Funding for CPRE comes from a variety of sources including: its status as one of the United States Department of Education's national research centers funded through the Office of Educational Research and Improvement (OERI); other federal contracts and grants; foundations; and direct work for individual states and school districts. The Finance Center is one component of CPRE's work and is headquartered at the University of Wisconsin under the direction of Allen Odden.

Jersey than in California (Picus and Fazal 1996; Odden, Monk, Nakib, and Picus 1995).

There are other limitations to the use of district-level data for analyzing educational organizations. Despite a general belief that more money will lead to better educational outcomes for students, research on the relationship between spending and student performance has been unable to conclusively establish a link between the two. It is possible the lack of detailed school-, classroom-, or student-level fiscal data is one of the reasons for the conflicting results reported in the literature to date (see, for example, Hanushek 1996 and Greenwald, Hedges, and Laine 1996a).

To understand how resources can best be used to improve a student's education, it seems important to know what resources are available to that child. At a minimum, a greater sense of what funds and services exist at the student's school will help inform such analyses. We often have student-specific information on a child's academic performance, demographic characteristics, and family income. Yet when we want to know how that child's performance is related to spending, we are forced to rely on district-level information. As shown above, district fiscal data show remarkable consistency across districts, potentially masking more significant differences in resource allocation and use at the school, classroom, or even student level. It is, of course, possible that school-level data collections will continue to show the same thing.

Site-based management is becoming more popular among educators and policymakers. This movement to devolve more authority and decision-making responsibility to school sites appears to be in line with current research trends in both education and the private sector. Many argue that if schools are to be managed successfully at the site level, and if states and districts are to hold schools accountable, more site-specific information will be needed (Odden and Busch 1998).

Even traditional equity analyses may suffer from the lack of school-level data. Hertert (1996) shows that there are substantial differences in per-pupil spending across schools within school districts and among schools across districts in California. If these expenditure differences exist in other states (and it is likely that

they do), then district-level data are inadequate even for traditional school-finance equity analysis.

The limitations described above suggest that school-level data
might provide better information and data on which to base future school-finance reform decisions, as well as on which to base
future accountability systems and reform efforts. Below, the potential advantages of school-level data collection are described.

Potential Uses of School-Level Data

A number of important insights into school-level data collection have been gleaned from the district- and school-level work
completed to date. This information is described in a series of
papers commissioned by the Finance Center of CPRE and published in a special issue of the *Journal of Education Finance* (Winter 1997). Since that work was completed, many others have
looked into the issues surrounding school-level data collection
and its use. Busch and Odden (1997), in summarizing the CPRE
commissioned papers, identified seven areas where school-level
data could be used to answer important questions. They include:

1. Governance

2. Accountability

3. Efficiency and productivity (effectiveness)

4. Equity

5. Adequacy

6. Comparability of data

7. Longitudinal analysis

This comprehensive list serves as an excellent guide to the
potential uses of school-level data. While others have created somewhat different lists of questions and potential benefits, all of them
fit under one of the seven categories listed above (see, for example, Herrington 1996; Guthrie 1998; Isaacs, Garet, and
Broughman 1998; Randall, Cooper, Speakman, and Rosenfield
1998). Each is described in more depth below.

Governance

In the 1990s, the focus of school management shifted from the district to the school. A number of policy or governance trends in education have resulted, including the push for site-based management,* charter schools, choice programs, and vouchers. In all instances, the driving force behind these proposed reforms is the school as the unit of concern and the location for decision-making and budget control. As schools grapple with the new reality of more authority and responsibility for student results, we need to be more attentive to the provision of timely, accurate school-level information. This information is needed by school managers seeking to provide educational services to their students, and by state policymakers concerned with holding schools accountable.

Despite the growing trend to argue for holding schools accountable for student outcomes, it is unlikely (and arguably wrong) to expect that the state will relinquish audit authority over the use of public school revenues by districts and schools. Particularly in a state like Washington—where a high percentage of total educational expenditures are funded by the state— legislators will always want assurances that the funds they appropriate for schools are used as expected and that actual expenditures match budget projections or estimates, with exceptions clearly documented and properly approved. Absent accurate reports of how public funds are spent, granting substantial decision-making authority to school sites is unlikely to occur as rapidly as proponents of site-based reforms would like to see.

Site-based management (SBM) is a commonly used term for a number of organizational options that have been implemented by school districts. Under traditional forms of school district governance, districts control most decision-making for all schools. SBM attempts to shift some of the authority for these decisions to the school site. Research has found that the three most common areas where power is devolved to school sites are personnel decisions, budgeting, and curriculum (see Odden and Busch 1998 for an excellent discussion of SBM). The nature of a school site's power, and the way that power is used or shared among the principal, teachers, and community varies from state to state and district to district.

Accountability

School-level data collection could play a major role in the design of future accountability systems. All 50 states have moved to improve educational accountability in recent years. Whether it is through school-site report cards, more intensive standardized testing, or detailed analyses of district spending, school performance is being looked at more closely than ever before. By linking spending, staff, and student data together at the school level, it might be possible to ascertain how different mixes of spending and/or staff affect student outcomes.

A related problem facing state policymakers is ensuring that the educational system, for which they still maintain overall responsibility, is meeting the needs of students, employers, and society generally. Rather than simply trust school-level decisions to be right, school-level data will give policymakers the ability to compare performance across schools, and to make sure all schools are allocating and using resources appropriately.

The last point brings up a distinction between holding schools accountable for what they do and controlling how they choose to do it. For example, site-based management argues that authority for most resource-allocation decisions should rest at the school. State accountability systems need not restrict that authority, but rather can be designed to ensure that the school can provide an accounting trail for the revenues and expenditures that meet the requirements of state law. School-level data systems are essential if school sites are to gain true decision-making autonomy.

Finally, Bush and Odden (1997) sum up the value of school-level data for accountability as follows:

> A school-level data system—that includes information on revenues or expenditures, personnel and personnel quality and expertise, other resource measures such as the enacted curriculum, and student achievement, especially changes in achievement over time—would allow site professionals and analysts to assess potential reasons for significant, or lack of, improvements in student achievement results, thus allowing an accountability system to be used intelligently rather than just descriptively or punitively.

Efficiency and Productivity (Effectiveness)

The efficient and productive or effective use of educational resources is of critical importance to the policy community. Several researchers have argued that school-level data would help us to better understand the observed 60/40 split described above (see page 79). They suggest that descriptive data at the school level would reveal how spending and resource utilization vary by grade level, type of school, program, and possibly by curricular area, if collected with these goals in mind (Farland 1997; Monk 1997). This information could be collected and analyzed to ascertain how policy drives school behavior (Busch and Odden 1997).

As many educators seek more funding for education, there are increasing calls for more efficient operation of schools, and for schools to show results in exchange for those additional funds. School-level data would also make it feasible for school decision-makers to conduct cost analyses of alternative programs and seek out the most cost-effective options for delivery of services. School-level data would allow analysts to determine which schools were making the greatest gains in student achievement per dollar spent and compare their programs and curriculum with other schools.

In addition to issues of efficiency, school-level data may be helpful in resolving questions surrounding productivity or effectiveness. Despite decades of research and literally thousands of studies attempting to link student outcomes with spending, the results to date have been inconclusive (Picus 1997b). Part of the problem is linking individual student data on achievement and characteristics with district-level data on expenditures. If data on expenditures were available at the school level, it might be possible to connect resources and student outcomes more clearly (Berne, Stiefel, and Moser 1997; Monk 1997; and Picus 1997a). Even if that connection remains elusive in the short term, it will be possible to develop a greater understanding of how different combinations of staff and other resources work to improve student performance under different circumstances. This will provide school leaders with more information about what programs are more likely to meet the needs of the children they serve.

Equity

The equitable distribution of resources has been the mainstay of school-finance research since Cubberley began writing about funding models in 1919. Yet until recently, the focus was always on the school district. Hertert (1996) shows that even in a state like California where substantial gains have been made in establishing horizontal equity in the school funding system, dramatic differences in per-pupil expenditures continue to exist across schools within the same district.* Few lawsuits have considered this issue, though the settlement in *Rodriguez v. Los Angeles Unified School District* in the late 1980s placed a great deal of emphasis on the equalization of spending on teacher salaries across schools in Los Angeles.

School-level equity analyses seem particularly well suited to a state like Washington where district-level horizontal—and, theoretically, vertical—equity has been largely achieved.** Are resource allocations equitable across schools in large districts? Do students have the same access to programs, teachers, and curriculum offerings throughout a district, or are there substantial differences in what schools are able to offer their children? It is in analyzing these important equity issues that school-level data may be the most crucial evidence.

One advantage of school-level data for equity analyses is that these data would allow policymakers to better measure revenues received by schools from nontraditional sources. For example, contributions from booster clubs, foundation grants, user fees, and associated student-body fund fees often generate substantial, and unequal, sums of revenue for schools. School-level fiscal data

---

Horizontal equity in school finance refers to the equal treatment of students. Typically horizontal equity is achieved when spending per pupil is roughly equal for all students with similar characteristics.

**Vertical equity* refers to the differential treatment of individuals with different characteristics. For example, it is generally accepted that children with disabilities require more expensive educational programs than do children who are not disabled. A vertically equitable system would provide additional funds for the education of children with disabilities. Horizontal equity would be maintained if all children with similar disabilities received roughly the same level of resources.

would allow us to better understand the implications of these nontraditional revenues on equity, across schools within a district and among schools across districts.

Adequacy

The 1990s have seen a resurgence in school-finance litigation. Since 1989, a total of 21 cases have found their way to the highest courts in their respective states. In 13 of those cases, the courts decided in favor of the plaintiffs. Beginning with the 1989 landmark decision in Kentucky,* courts have been more willing to overthrow the existing funding system, define remedies, and establish concrete requirements for constitutional remedy. In many instances, these decisions have focused on an additional factor beyond equity in school finance—adequacy. Adequacy cases argue that it is the responsibility of the state to provide an "adequate" level of resources to ensure each child receives a satisfactory education. As envisioned by William Clune (1994), adequacy shifts the focus of school-finance reform from inputs to an emphasis on high minimum outcomes. Although this may sound simple on the surface, it represents a major change in the way states—and consequently school districts—will think about school funding issues in the future.

Defining adequacy requires accurate information on what schools spend to provide educational services to children, and how those resources vary with differing student needs. It may be that the best place to collect the information needed to assess adequacy is at the school site (*see* Farland 1997; Monk 1997; and Picus 1999). School-level data will make it easier to understand what it costs to provide an adequate education to the average student, and provide a better basis for funding students with special needs.

In addition, Farland (1997) has suggested that it will be possible for state departments of education and local school districts to more accurately estimate the costs of new or proposed programs if they have better information on the costs of running schools and the various component programs they operate.

---

*Rose v. Council for Better Education, 790 S.W.2d 186 (1989).

Comparability

A state-level effort to collect uniform school-level data would go a long way toward resolving differences in the way districts account for school-level resources—at least within individual states. Today state data-collection systems vary from nonexistent to highly detailed accounting systems that allow schools to sort financial data by site, program and/or activity (function), as well as object code. Unfortunately, even within individual states there are substantial differences in how school-level data are reported to districts. Another problem is the accuracy and consistency with which expenditures are coded by district staff. As a result, it is often not possible to make comparisons across districts.

Various states have begun to implement school-level data systems using new software programs to improve data comparability. Speakman and others (1997) show that a great deal of comparable data can be produced quite quickly using In$ight, a program developed by Coopers and Lybrand that is designed to allocate school resources to one of five categories. In theory, In$ight provides a reporting system combined with a relational database, enabling analysis of expenditures by program across school and district sites. South Carolina, which is using a similar system to collect school-level data from its school districts, has recently entered into a contract with IBM to develop a data system to allow state education decision-makers and policymakers to use these data.

Oregon has begun an ambitious program to create a statewide chart of accounts that must be used by all school districts. When complete, school-level fiscal data will be available for all schools and potentially for some curriculum areas at the high school level. At present, Oregon does not have a standard chart of accounts at the district level.

Other states that have school-level data systems in place include Texas and Ohio. Hawaii, which is unique among the fifty states in that there is only one, state-operated school district, is also moving to develop a better school-level accounting and reporting system, and a number of districts in Utah have begun using the aforementioned In$ight system.

Longitudinal Analysis

One of the weaknesses of much of the research on the impact of educational resources on student performance is the use of cross-sectional data. Rarely are data available for multiple-year periods, and when they are, there is often so much variation in how they were collected from year to year that longitudinal analyses are impossible. Picus (1997a) argues that the consistent collection of school-level data over time would allow researchers to conduct longitudinal analyses that would fill the gaps found so far in these production-function studies. It should be pointed out that dis-trict-level data could also be used for longitudinal studies.

Issues to Resolve in the Collection of School-Level Data

States that collect school-level data have run into a number of significant problems in the design and implementation of their systems. This section summarizes the many potential pitfalls fac-ing the development of a useful school-level data system. Prob-lems ranging from use of the data to protecting privacy, as well as accuracy and system comparability and capacity, must all be ad-dressed if the data collected are to be useful to state and local decision-makers.

Cost and Administrative Burden

Perhaps the most important consideration in designing a school-level data system is determining whether the value of the data collected will be worth the cost. In July 1998 at the NCES data-collectors conference in Washington, DC, Matthew Cohen indicated that Ohio has spent an estimated $250 million on its school-level information systems in the last 11 years. This in-cludes costs to both the state and to local school districts in com-plying with state requirements.

Oregon has estimated that establishing its new school-level data system will cost as much as $6 million, and has appropriated $2.9 million to date for this effort. This figure only represents the costs to the state, and does not include the substantial costs to be incurred by districts in shifting to the new accounting system and training their staff in its use.

Collection of school-level data by the state will place an additional administrative burden on school administrators at the district and school levels. This burden will result in considerable costs to schools either through the need to hire additional staff or through lost opportunities to do other things at the school site due to the time spent complying with the requirements of the data system.

Making the Data Useful

If school-level data are collected, they must be useful to policymakers, school officials at the state and local levels, and hopefully to researchers. Absent some way to use these data for improving the education system in a state, there is little reason to collect them. Busch and Odden (1997) argue that any state-level data system must include microdata that are integrated, connected, and multidimensional and that can be combined in any way desired through a relational database. To be truly useful to state administrators, local school officials, researchers, and others, the system needs to be designed to allow users to aggregate and configure data in ways they choose.

Beyond that, it is important that schools and school districts report their data accurately. Both Farland (1997) and Goertz (1997) suggest that an incentive to get school sites to report fiscal and staffing data accurately would be to tie state funding directly to the school site.

Lack of Comparability

One of the major problems analysts have found in looking at school-level data has been lack of comparability across districts. Many states have large computer cooperatives that provide data-processing services to school districts. Often these cooperatives allow districts to use individually designed reporting systems, and then the cooperatives establish translation tables to create required state reports. Since most states only require district-level data, this simply requires aggregation of school-level data regardless of the form. This method serves districts well, since most districts want a standard system for all their member schools. However, because of the variation in the way districts choose to use the cooperative's capabilities, it is unlikely these cooperatives would be able to provide comparable school-level data for all their member districts. In short, the cooperatives support idiosyncratic school-level reporting but maintain the ability to generate district-level summaries that meet state requirements. Finding consistent school-level data through such systems is problematic.

Related to this is the need for the state to establish common reporting standards (Speakman and others 1997). Absent consistent accounting classifications and standard definitions of personnel assignments, comparisons across schools will be of limited value. As part of a systematic coding structure, the state would need to provide accurate guidelines for classification of expenditures and staff so school and district officials have the knowledge to place items in the proper category.

Another issue that would need to be considered in school-level equity analyses is property wealth. School-finance equity analyses almost always focus on the relationship between wealth and spending. Most schools do not have their own tax base or taxable wealth on which to levy a tax. Consequently, it would not be possible to conduct analyses that compare wealth. It would only be possible to determine how spending or revenue levels varied across schools. Even if school-level wealth measures could be identified, Berne, Stiefel, and Moser (1997) argue that student mobility within districts would make accurate measurement of that wealth nearly impossible.

Defining a School

Establishing a clear definition of a school is a difficult task. There are literally hundreds of different school organization models in existence in each of the states and across the nation. For example, what is an elementary school? Most educate children in grades K-5, but some are K-6 or K-8, or in states where kindergarten is not mandatory, there may be schools that serves grades 1-5, or 1-6, and so forth. Many districts have elected to establish primary centers, meaning an elementary-age child might attend grades K-2 at one school and 3-5 at another. There is, of course, nothing sacred about those grade distinctions either.

High schools are typically designed to serve children in grades 9-12 or 10-12, but in some smaller communities there are secondary schools that serve children in grades 7-12. Moreover, in many school districts there are other combinations of secondary schools. Perhaps the most difficult to identify are intermediate schools. Generally called middle or junior high schools, intermediate schools contain any number of combinations of grades from 4 through 9 or even 10. While the most common are grades 6-8, other organizational structures are found consistently among school districts.

Beyond defining schools, there are many new institutions that need to be considered. Charter schools, choice and voucher programs, private operators of public schools such as the Edison Project, and home schooling combine to make defining a school a complex task. Designing a school-level data system that can accommodate the many different types and forms of schools is clearly a complex task.

Complexity

One of the major problems with state accounting systems is their complexity. Ohio has account strings that are 32 characters long (Cohen 1997), and Minnesota's are 17 characters (Farland 1997). While these allow for many different ways to sort and aggregate data, they also increase the probability of mistakes or misclassification of entries. Account codes typically include a number of digits for each component of the entire string. This allows for more detailed classification of expenditures as more of the available digits are used. Often some of the digits are optional, allowing the district or school some flexibility in how they are used, whereas other digits are required and the types of expenditures coded with those digits carefully prescribed.

Infrastructure, Technology, and Training

Once data systems are created, states need to be sure districts and schools have the capacity to report the data required. This will likely require upgrading of school and district hardware and software, as well as substantial training for staff, particularly school-level staff for whom such reporting is new. Oregon is finding that a great deal of training is necessary to ensure that expenditures and revenues are coded consistently by everyone.

In addition, the state must have the capacity to receive and process all the data collected. For example, Florida collects a wide range of student data five times a year. Each collection has as many as 100 student variables for each of the 3 million students in the state. Given five separate collection points, there is the potential for 15 million student records and as many as 1.5 billion data elements a year. All these need to be stored, processed, and made available to system users.

Moreover, links between this massive student database and the staff and fiscal data must also be maintained. Florida has installed a data terminal at each school in the state to facilitate electronic submission of the required reports (Herrington 1996; Nakib 1996). Developing the capacity to handle the massive quantity of data collected is crucial to the success of any school-level data system.

As documented by both Hertert (1996) and Picus (1997a), the development of a database with school-level fiscal data in California was a complex and time-consuming task. In the end, researchers were forced to collect hard-copy data from school districts and key punch the information themselves. This process took over 9 months to complete and resulted in the input of over 18,000 pages of data, all for just 30 of the state's 1,000 districts. The collection of school-level revenue and/or expenditure data would resolve this problem. Moreover, Berne, Stiefel, and Moser (1997) argue that good fiscal, staff, curriculum, and assessment data at the school level would help in the analysis of vertical equity issues as well.

Privacy

Picus (1997a) describes the problems CPRE researchers had in seeking permission to use Florida's student database due to concerns over individual privacy rights. In the case of CPRE's Florida research, the problem was not resolved until the department head holding up approval left the state to take a job elsewhere.

Privacy is a legitimate concern, and it is important that school-level data systems be designed to ensure that individual student data elements are properly protected. The NCES addresses this problem by offering site licenses to organizations that wish to look at databases with individually identifiable data. The license establishes certain criteria for how the data can be used, and how they should be stored and protected at all times. Data tapes and CD-ROMs must be returned to NCES when no longer in use, and the government conducts random audits of license holders to ensure they are meeting the terms of the license agreement. Violation of the terms of the license can result in fines and jail sentences. Some form of protection needs to be established for state databases with individually identifiable data as well.

How Have Researchers Used School-Level Data?

In considering the relative merits of a school-level data-collection effort, it is helpful to understand how others have used similar data in the past. To date, there has been little research using school-level databases despite the potential richness of the information that is available. Three types of studies were identified in developing this chapter: those using federal databases like the Schools and Staffing Survey (SASS), those using state-maintained school-level databases, and those done through the construction of school-district-specific school-level databases.

Studies Using Federal Data

One of the earliest attempts to look at school-level data was the work of Picus (1993a and 1993b). By merging data from the

SASS with Census Bureau data on governmental expenditures, Picus was able to estimate spending patterns at the school level. Because fiscal data were not available at the school level, the analysis focused on the use of staff. Particularly interesting in these analyses was the difference between the estimated pupil/teacher ratio and the teacher self-reported class size. Picus found that while the average pupil/teacher ratio reported in schools was in the vicinity of 16.5 or 17.1, self-reported class sizes ranged from 24 to 32 (Picus and Bhimani 1993; Picus1994b) or from 50 to 100 percent higher than even school-level statistics indicated.

Two important findings emerged from this work. First, it is clear that many individuals classified as "teachers" in our public school systems have assignments other than spending the full day in the classroom. Second, it appears that as the size of the district increases, and as its wealth declines, the disparity between the calculated pupil/teacher ratio and the actual class size grows. Further school-level analyses were not possible with the SASS and Census data.

Studies Using State Data

Early work in assessing school-level spending patterns was done by CPRE researchers in Florida, California, and New York. In Florida, Nakib (1996) assessed the use of resources at the school level. He concluded that when analyzed on the basis of district size, total expenditures, district wealth, percentage of minority students, and low-income students, there was little variation in spending patterns by object, function, or program at the district and at the school level. Nakib was not sure of the cause of these similarities, wondering if the uniform reporting requirements Florida placed on schools and districts were the cause of this consistency in findings. In his conclusion, Nakib wondered, if spending patterns were similar, what other factors led to differences in school effectiveness? Additional school-level variables might lead to the answer to this question.

In California, Hertert (1996) analyzed school-level equity, finding that despite the substantial district-level equity in the distribution of general resources to education, there were substantial variations in the amount of money spent per pupil across schools within districts and among schools across districts. In addition, she found that pupil/teacher ratios were very consistent across school districts and schools, though there was substantial variation in what types of courses were offered in high schools by those teachers. Variation in the number of advanced math and science courses, for example, could explain why graduates of some schools perform better in these subjects than do graduates of other schools.

In New York, Monk, Roelke, and Brent (1996) found that while spending patterns tended to be similar across districts and even schools, the use of personnel varied considerably, with some schools devoting substantially more resources to high-level academic courses than other schools. Clearly the potential of these differences to affect the level of student learning is important to understanding how resources matter, even if the focus is on teacher qualifications and what they are teaching rather than how much they cost.

Sherman, Best, and Luskin (1996) conducted a study of the potential uses of school-level data sets in Ohio and Texas. Many of their findings were similar to those of district-level research reported above, confirming the consistency of spending patterns among schools. While Sherman, Best, and Luskin found differences in the levels of expenditures for various functions across schools, they found that there was little difference in the share of total expenditures spent on instruction, administration, and support services.

Recently, Jay Chambers (1998) analyzed Ohio's school-level data in an attempt to estimate the costs of special education. He was able to make a number of important estimates of the costs attributable to services provided for children with disabilities. The information he provided is highly policy-relevant in understanding how much is spent for special education and what that money buys. Its potential value in other states is very high, though it was Chambers's view that if national estimates were to be attempted, it would be necessary to collect information from each of the states individually. The analysis would be very difficult for those states, such as Ohio, that did not have state-level data.

The collection of school-level data is a relatively new venture. To date, there has been limited use by researchers of the information collected by Florida, Ohio, and Texas (the states with the most advanced school-level data-collection systems). To a large extent, particularly in Texas, the data are used to provide citizens with a great deal of detailed information on their local schools. To date there has been limited analysis of what those data mean, either by researchers or policymakers. Chambers's work with the Ohio data provides detailed estimates of the costs and personnel allocations for special education in Ohio. The data give a clearer picture of special-education costs than has been previously available, and enables state-level officials to compare costs of the same services across schools and school districts.

With further refinement, school-level data collections on finance, personnel, and student characteristics may make it possible to gain a better understanding of how money (and other resources) matter in improving student performance. Policymakers would be interested in these data both to better understand these links, and to help develop measures of the cost-effectiveness of alternative educational strategies and their relative effectiveness with children from different backgrounds and locations.

Studies Using School-Level Data from District Databases

A number of studies have been conducted using databases with school-level data constructed from individual district records. Miles's (1995) study of Boston showed that if all individuals in the district classified as teachers were placed in regular classrooms, class size could be reduced from an average of 22 to 13. While this change may not really be possible due to the need to provide special services to children with severe disabilities, Miles also provided a number of different policy options showing how the average class size would vary as some of the district's current special-education practices were continued. Her analysis provided information that a school board could use to make policy decisions on class size and the delivery of special education.

Recently, a number of researchers have conducted a major study of school-level resource allocation in four urban school districts in the United States—Rochester, New York City, Chicago, and Fort Worth. In their introduction to a special issue of the *Journal of Education Finance* devoted to this work, Goertz and Stiefel (1998) focus on three things:

- Intradistrict fiscal equity
- Decision-making processes
- Considerations for implementation of school-level databases

A number of factors take on heightened importance when school-level equity is considered.

- School-level analyses can lead to public comparisons among local schools leading to potential conflicts between the goals of horizontal and vertical equity. Some schools may appear to have more resources than others due to the special needs of the children at the school. While this meets the traditional goal of vertical equity, it may appear unfair to parents of other nearby schools who only see that their school does not have as many resources available to them as does the school with the children with special needs.

- Local constituents don't always understand differences between per-pupil positions and per-pupil expenditures. Differences in salaries of teachers could lead to lower teacher costs per pupil at schools with relatively more teachers, confounding analyses that rely on expenditures and pupil/teacher ratios.

- In all four of the districts studied, school-based budgeting takes place only at the margins, with relatively little real discretionary authority allocated to the school sites. Moreover, it is generally the principal who has the most power in making those fiscal decisions that are possible at the school site. It is critical to specify clearly who is ultimately responsible for the academic and fiscal performance of the school. Where this is not clear, conflicts between site councils and the principal have arisen.

- Data on dollars, positions, outcomes, and demographics should be integrated into one database. Districts typically keep these data in different databases. It is typically difficult, if not impossible, to merge the data on students, teach-ers, and spending into one, unified database. By maintain-ing all these data in one, easily accessible data system, com-parisons across students and schools will be facilitated.

In addition to this work, Bruce Cooper and teams of analysts from Coopers and Lybrand have collected and analyzed a great deal of data from New York City Schools and other districts throughout the country. The initial "cascade" model developed by Cooper and others (1994) attempted to track funds starting at the central-office level as they "cascaded" down to the local schools. The model has been revised over time and is now available to school districts through Coopers and Lybrand under the name In$ight. The model divides expenditures into ten categories, five each at the district and school levels. At each level the same five functions are specified:

- Administration
- Operations and facilities
- Teacher support
- Pupil support
- Instruction

The findings from Cooper's model when applied to eight school districts across the country showed that central-office ex-penditures consumed between 6 and 20 percent of district expen-ditures, leaving between 80 and 94 percent for the schools. The model forms the basis of the Ohio school-level data collection, and a variation of it is in use today in South Carolina as well. Cooper (1998) indicates that Hawaii is looking into the use of the In$ight model to track expenditures in the schools that are part of that statewide school system.

Conclusion

Collecting fiscal, staffing, and student data from increasingly smaller and more disaggregated levels of the school system makes the task more and more complex. As the pyramid in figure 5.1 shows, a state-level data system has only 51 data-collection points—the 50 states plus the District of Columbia. District-level data systems have over 15,000 data-collection points, while a national school-level data system would require collecting information from over 80,000 individual schools. Because of differences in reporting requirements—both district and state—as well as the potential for data-entry errors at each level, comparing information across units, be they schools, districts, or states, is difficult.

The complexity of collecting data on educational resource allocation and use is confirmed by the difficulty NCES had in developing a cross-walk to enable it to report state-level school finance consistently across the 50 states. In the end, only 39 states were successfully included in the cross-walk due to the difficulties of finding ways to compare individual state systems. As the number of entities included in the database increases, the complexity grows. Although this problem may be mitigated somewhat by the ability of a state to force districts to accept a standard reporting system, the problem is still immense.

Figure 5.1

The Data-Collection Pyramid

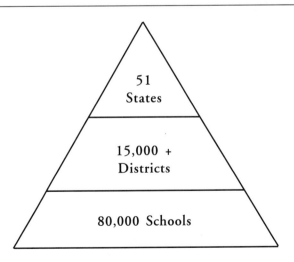

Assuming a state is willing to undertake the expense of developing a school-level data system, it gains a wealth of information that can help state and local decision-makers understand how the schools of that state operate and how schools translate resource-allocation decisions into student outcomes. Moreover, it can help states develop accountability standards for the schools, making it possible to know immediately which schools are succeeding and which need assistance.

Despite all the potential for school-level data, it is not certain that once the data are collected we will be able to answer all the questions we have or that we could pose. Recent research in Ohio has shown that once people understand what the data system can provide, they want more capabilities. Continuing to refine and upgrade any data-collection system is both important and costly. Berne, Stiefel, and Moser (1997) state that while many different school-level data-collection efforts have recently begun, at some point it will be "important to use cost-benefit principles in deciding what kinds of uniform data to gather across schools in a city, state, or the country."

Data collection is a valuable activity only if it is accompanied by clear, well-thought-out analyses using those data. Each state legislature generally wants to know that the funds it appropriates are being well used, but the quality of school data available at present is generally inadequate to fulfill this purpose. Most data collection to date has been restricted to district-level data, and the analyses have been narrowly focused rather than comprehensive.

CHAPTER 6

Conclusion:
Components of a Productive System

The evidence presented in the preceding chapters makes it difficult to reach a strong conclusion whether and how money matters in improving student performance. Even though virtually all educators believe that additional resources will lead to higher student performance, the knowledge is still incomplete on how best to spend dollars to achieve our goal. As a result, demands for more money, absent a well-reasoned description of how the money will be used, do not build confidence that the money—by itself—will make a difference.

Hanushek (1994a, 1997) argues that the proper incentives for better performance and efficient use of educational resources are not in place, and that a system that holds schools accountable for student performance is essential to the more effective use of existing and new money.

Improving student performance, with or without new funds, requires four ingredients:

- Reallocation of existing resources
- Incentives for improved performance
- Development of the concept of "venture capital" for schools and school systems
- A more market-based budgeting environment

Each is described in more detail below.

Reallocation of Existing Resources

Regardless of what impact additional funds might have, it is important that existing resources be used as efficiently as possible. In her study of the Boston school district, Miles (1995) found that if all individuals classified as teachers were to teach classes of equal size, the average class in the district could have been reduced from 22 to 13 students. While this would have placed all children with disabilities in regular programs, Miles also provided estimates of what the average class size would be if some of the most severely disabled children continued to receive services under current programs. Dramatic class-size reductions were still possible.

Miles's work highlights the fact that in many districts it may be possible to further reduce class size through different assignments of teachers throughout the district. To the extent that smaller class size improves student performance, these changes would offer an improvement in student performance at little or no cost.

Odden and Busch (1998) argue that schools can find the additional funds (which range from $82,000 to $349,000 per school per year) to finance the various New American Schools designs through a combination of creative use of categorical funds, elimination of classroom aides, and reallocation of resources, such as the elimination of one or two teaching positions. While some of these options may result in larger classes, or fewer teachers, the more intensive use of staff and greater professional development activities available seem to result in improved student performance in many of the schools that have adopted these designs.

Before seeking additional funds, there may be ways to restructure what is done with current funds. Accelerated Schools, the New American Schools program designs, and hard analyses of current staffing patterns could all yield improved student performance.

Incentives

The use of incentives to improve school performance is not a new idea. Unfortunately, the incentives that seem to have the most success are sanctions. Schools faced with threats of intervention often act quickly to improve performance rather than risk the stigma of a sanction. Conversely, many positive incentives have been less successful. For example, high-performing schools are often granted waivers from state regulation in exchange for success. In this case, the regulatory system loosened constraints that may have made the system successful. Perhaps the more appropriate incentive would be to provide such waivers to underperforming schools with the hope that increased flexibility would lead to improvements.

Hanushek (1997) argues that the incentives currently in place in schools need to be changed because they do not encourage teachers to work to improve student performance. He suggests that there is not sufficient awareness of positive performance incentives, and that more experimentation and research are needed.

Venture Capital (Equity)

In a study of the costs of implementing California's "Caught in the Middle" reforms for middle schools, Marsh and Sevilla (1992) found that the annual costs of restructuring schools to meet the requirements of this program were between 3 and 6 percent higher than current average expenditures per pupil in California schools. They also concluded that the first-year startup costs amounted to approximately 25 percent of annual costs.

The problem schools face is finding those startup funds. For example, in a large district with 10 middle schools, each with a budget of $10 million, the initial startup costs would be $25 million, a figure that would be hard to find in a district budget. However, if the program were started in two schools a year, the annual cost would be only $5 million. Since the money would be for startup purposes only, once the $5 million was appropriated the first year, it could be transferred to two different schools each year until all 10 schools had implemented the program. Then, the district would have $5 million to put to some other good use.

Related to the concept of venture capital are *revolving funds*. This is a concept that offers a way for school districts to deal with large purchases that occur on a regular, but non-annual basis, like computers. The average computer purchased for use in a school probably has a useful life of three to five years. Many schools are unable to replace their computers on that short a timetable. As a result, there are a lot of schools that continue to use old Apple IIe and similar vintage computers.

As described above, budget procedures in school districts do not reward schools for saving resources in one year to make large purchases the next year. A school that receives a sum of discretionary money in one year is likely to lose any of the funds it has not expended by the end of the fiscal year. As a result, schools are often unable to make a large coordinated purchase of computers and associated equipment at one time.

A solution to this would be a revolving fund in the district to pay for such purchases. Suppose a district with eight elementary schools wants to support a computer lab of 25 stations in each school. It estimates that each lab's computers need to be replaced once every four years, and in today's dollars the cost of replacing the entire lab is approximately $70,000. Assuming the district had found one-time funds to establish the labs, it would probably try to provide each school with equal annual funding for replacement of computers. This solution is generally used in districts in an attempt to provide equitable funding to each school. The cost of this would be $140,000 (0.25 x $70,000 x 8). In this case, however, equitable funding has a significant drawback: Since this funding is only enough to replace one quarter of the computers each year (a four-year replacement cycle), schools would find themselves with four different computer versions in each lab all the time.

An alternative would be to establish a revolving fund of $140,000 a year. This fund could be used to completely replace the labs in two schools each year, thus establishing a four-year replacement cycle and ensuring that each school's computing facility is equipped with similar computers. It is likely that under these circumstances the labs would function more smoothly with fewer problems related to the difficulties of networking different computers with different capabilities. Schools would know exactly when the computers in their labs were to be replaced. Moreover, though capital spending across the eight schools would not be equitable on a year-to-year basis, equity over the lifetime of the computers in the labs would be maintained.

The revolving fund could also be applied to the provision of professional development services and other school-reform efforts that require one-time or non-annual expenditures. One problem in education today is that once funds are appropriated to a school or program, they become the possession of that entity. Finding a way to use the money in a revolving fashion would facilitate continued improvements in educational programs. The major problem is determining who gets the venture-capital funds first and who has to wait. Today in many large districts, the superintendent publishes lists of the best and worst performing schools, and such lists could be used to prioritize the allocation of these funds. Another issue is the equity of the distribution. While some schools will get more one year than others, over the established time period all schools will receive the funds, so one simply has to accept the idea that equity is measured over some time frame, and not on an annual basis.

Market Approaches

Many of today's reformers call for market-based changes in the organization of our schools. There are many ways to introduce the market into the educational arena, but most of these fall in one way or another under the heading of school choice. Public school choice can be considered as either intradistrict or interdistrict choice, and these can be broken down further into the various types of programs in each category. Two other types of choice involve the blurring of the line between public and private education: private school vouchers and privatization of former public schools. Each of these will be discussed in turn.

Intradistrict choice programs, by definition confined to one school district, grew largely out of an attempt to desegregate schools rather than to provide competition or parent choice. The first of these programs is called *controlled choice*, where districts created models for assigning students to schools outside of the traditional neighborhood school model as a way of reducing segregation (Rouse and McLaughlin 1999).

A second type of intradistrict choice program is the *magnet school*. Magnet schools were designed to attract white students to schools with high minority populations, often located in heavily minority communities. Magnet schools can be either entire schools with specialized education programs or specialized education programs within regular schools. Studies have shown that magnet schools are effective in reducing segregation (Blank, Levine, and Steel 1996). While desegregation was the driving force behind the development of magnet schools, such schools have introduced more choice, and competition, into the educational arena.

The newest model of intradistrict choice is the *charter school*. With the development of the charter school, the purpose of the choice models shifts away from desegregation to a focus on providing parents with the choice to send their children to schools that may be less regulated than their traditional neighborhood school. These schools operate under a charter between those who organize the school (typically teachers and parents) and a sponsor (typically the local school board or state board of education).

Charter schools may provide specialized education programs or they may offer a regular education program, but the lack of regulatory constraints allows them to deliver it in innovative ways. For example, the school has more control over important issues such as hiring and budgeting, and often this control is shared with the parents as well. While the theory is that having control over hiring practices may allow these schools to hire a select staff that can positively affect student achievement, more research needs to be done to ascertain whether those effects actually exist. The same is true for the theory that charter schools stimulate creative innovations in education that positively influence student achievement. While some anecdotal evidence suggests that this is the case, more research must be done to determine the impact on student achievement.

Interdistrict choice programs allow the transfer of students between school districts. Although interdistrict choice programs also grew out of attempts to desegregate, they always had the goal of increasing parental choice as well. Many states allow interdistrict choice through *open enrollment* policies, which vary from state to state. Some states mandate that all districts have open enrollment, while others allow districts to choose whether they wish to be open or closed. By the 1993-94 school year, open enrollment was the most common school-choice program in this country. Twenty-nine percent of school districts had open enrollment compared to only 14 percent of districts with intradistrict choice (National Center for Education Statistics 1996). By 1997, 18 states had some form of open-enrollment legislation. However, participation in such programs is still quite low (Rouse and McLauglin 1999).

As with intradistrict programs, many theorize that this injection of competition into education will improve its quality. This may be more probable with this type of choice because of the potential for districts to compete with each other. However, giving parents the opportunity to choose the district in which their child is enrolled may serve to weaken the link between district/ school quality and residents, perhaps causing a reduction in investment in the local school system. As was previously mentioned, the number of children participating in open enrollment is limited, and these potential collateral effects have not yet been observed or studied.

Perhaps the most talked-about form of choice program is the *voucher program.* Voucher programs can be organized in different ways, but the basic idea is to give some children access to private schools by issuing vouchers to their families, which the families then give to the school in lieu of a tuition payment. Often these programs have the intention of allowing low-income students to go to schools they could not otherwise afford to attend, though vouchers are not necessarily limited to those in poverty. These provisions depend on the particular voucher system in place at the state or local level.

While the idea of vouchers is not new, such programs are still relatively limited. In 1990, Wisconsin became the first state to implement a program that provides vouchers for low-income students to attend nonsectarian private schools in Milwaukee (Witte, Sterr, and Thorn 1995). This program has since been changed to include parochial schools as well (Witte 1998). Ohio adopted a similar program in 1996, one that allows students to attend both sectarian and nonsectarian private schools (Greene, Howell, and Peterson 1997).

To date, a limited number of voucher programs have been evaluated. Witte's (1998) evaluation of the Milwaukee Voucher Experiment produced mixed findings. On the one hand, parents were pleased with the choice program, especially in contrast to the schools their children attended before receiving the voucher that allowed them to transfer to another school. The fact that parents were happier with the schools their children attend also led to greater parental involvement. On the other hand, the effect on these children's test scores was not as dramatic as the program's creators might have hoped. In many cases, test score gains were similar for students in the choice program and those who were still enrolled in the Milwaukee Public School System. In addition, three private schools closed midyear, creating upheaval for the families whose children attended these schools.

It is important to consider the complicated context from which these findings are taken, but Witte's conclusions do not support the argument that the competition provided by choice will positively affect student achievement. On the other hand, Greene, Peterson, and Du (1997) reanalyzed Witte's data using different controls and statistical procedures and concluded that student test scores did rise in Milwaukee voucher schools. The different findings led to considerable debate. Clearly more research is needed, perhaps on larger voucher experiments. At this point, however, it is safe to say that "the verdict is still out" on the impact of voucher programs on student achievement.

The last market-based approach that will be discussed here is the *privatization* of schools that were formerly public. This is also a relatively new approach, and one that arose largely out of a demand for strategies that could save failing schools. The argument is that if public education functions like a monopoly (a firm that has control over its price and product), because it is not subject to competition, it has little incentive to function efficiently. By introducing some competition through privatization, schools would be forced to provide higher quality education at a lower price.

Privatization in the education sector typically involves contracting out services. And while some services (such as food service) are contracted out in many public schools, the issue here is school boards and school districts that have contracted with private companies to run entire schools. Companies like The Edison Project and EAI (Education Alternatives, Inc.) form an agreement with a district whereby they receive the money that the public school would be getting for the children who attend the school, and run the school using their own methods. Ostensibly, these methods can raise student achievement even while operating at a lower cost.

The Edison Project has been evaluated to determine whether these effects indeed occur and the results seem promising (The Edison Project, 1998). However, just as with the previous approaches that have been discussed here, not enough research has been done to know what the long-term effect will be of allowing private companies to run public institutions. There are a number of philosophical questions that must be addressed. For example, if The Edison Project is successful at running the school at a lower cost than what the district (taxpayers) pays them, should private stockholders profit from this efficiency? This and other questions will have to be answered if companies like Edison continue to form such agreements with public school entities.

While there are many ways of inciting competition in education, choice programs tend to be the most controversial and therefore get the most attention. Those who oppose choice programs have a number of objections. Probably the most common one is that while the introduction of market competition in education is supposed to improve the quality of education, this will only happen for a select group of children, thereby leaving the others with either the same poor-quality education or worse. Opponents argue that competition means the good schools will thrive and the bad schools will shut down, but this is unlikely, particularly in large, overcrowded urban districts. More likely, students whose families have the resources, time, or acumen to work the system might get into the better schools, while others will not.

Picus (1994b) suggests market-type mechanisms are needed within school systems. He argues that for markets to succeed, failure is an essential ingredient. Since it is unlikely schools will close (or fail), a proxy for that failure is needed. He suggests that schools be given more authority over the use of their resources and be held accountable for student outcomes. Schools implementing successful programs will meet their goals; those selecting inappropriate programs most likely will fall short of those goals. Providers of unsuccessful programs will go out of business—leading to the failure that is part of a market—and providers of successful programs will thrive, be they school districts, consortia of school personnel, or private companies.

Picus goes on to suggest that the market for teachers within a district be made less restrictive, with principals seeking teachers who share their management style and programmatic vision.

Market mechanisms are a powerful tool for improving the performance of an organization, but current models for market structures in public education have not yet been fully evaluated. This has lead to an environment of uncertainty for the public and policymakers alike. Until more research can be completed, the long-term effects on student achievement, as well as broader issues, are unclear. Picus's suggestions are designed to provide the incentives of a market but avoid much of the resistance and uncertainty frequently associated with them.

Bibliography

Adams, J. E. "Spending School Reform Dollars in Kentucky: Familiar Patterns and New Programs, but Is This Reform?" *Educational Evaluation and Policy Analysis* 16, 4 (1994): 375-90.

Alexander, Arthur J. *Teachers, Salaries and School District Expenditures.* Santa Monica, California: The Rand Corporation, 1974.

Allington, Richard.L., and Peter Johnston. "Coordination, Collaboration, and Consistency: The Redesign of Compensatory and Special Education Interventions." In *Effective Programs for Students At Risk,* edited by Robert E. Slavin, Nancy L. Karweit, and Nancy A. Madden. 320-54. Needham Heights, Massachusetts: Allyn & Bacon, 1989.

Barro, S. M. *What Does the Education Dollar Buy? Relationships of Staffing, Staff Characteristics, and Staff Salaries to State Per-Pupil Spending.* Washington, DC: SMB Economic Research, 1992.

Barro, Stephen M., and Stephen J. Carroll. *Budget Allocation by School Districts: An Analysis of Spending for Teachers and Other Resources.* Santa Monica, California: The Rand Corporation, 1975.

Bell, J. D. "Smaller = Better?" *State Legislatures* (June 1998). http://www.ncsl.org/programs/educ/class.htm

Berne, R.; L. Stiefel; and M. Moser. "The Coming of Age of School-Level Finance Data." *Journal of Education Finance* 22, 3 (1997): 246-54.

Betts, J. R. "Does School Quality Matter? Evidence from the National Longitudinal Survey of Youth." *Review of Economics and Statistics* 77 (May 1995): 231-50.

_____ . "Is There a Link Between School Inputs and Earnings? Fresh Scrutiny of an Old Literature." In *Does Money Matter?,* edited by Gary Burtless. 141-91. Washington, DC: Brookings Institution Press, 1996.

Betts, J. R.; K. S. Rueben; and A. Danenberg. *Equal Resources, Equal Outcomes? The Distribution of School Resources and Student Achievement in California*. San Francisco, California: Public Policy Institute of California, 2000.

Blank, Rolf K.; Roger E. Levine; and Lauri Steel. "After 15 Years: Magnet Schools in Urban Education." In *Who Chooses? Who Loses? Culture, Institutions, and the Unequal Effects of School Choice*, edited by Bruce Fuller and Richard F. Elmore (with Gary Orfield). New York: Teachers College Press, 1996.

Bobbitt, Sharon A., and Marilyn Miles McMillen. "Teacher Training, Certification, and Assignment." Paper presented to the annual meeting of the American Educational Research Association, Boston, Massachusetts, 1990.

Brewer, D.; C. Krop; B. P. Gill; and R. Reichardt. "Estimating the Cost of National Class Size Reductions Under Different Policy Alternatives." *Educational Evaluation and Policy Analysis* 21, 2 (1999): 179-92.

Burtless, G. "Introduction and Summary." In *Does Money Matter?*, edited by Gary Burtless. 1-42. Washington, DC: Brookings Institution Press, 1996.

Busch, C., and A. Odden. "Introduction to the Special Issue: Improving Educational Policy and Results with School-Level Data: A Synthesis of Multiple Perspectives." *Journal of Education Finance* 22, 3 (1997): 225-45.

Card, D., and A. B. Krueger. "Does School Quality Matter? Returns to Education and the Characteristics of Public Schools in the United States." *Journal of Political Economy* 100 (February 1992a): 1-40.

_____ . "School Quality and Black-White Relative Earnings: A Direct Assessment." *Quarterly Journal of Economics* 107 (February 1992b): 151-200.

_____ . "The Economic Return to School Quality." In *Assessing Educational Practices: The Contribution of Economics*, edited by W. Baumol and W. Becker. 161-82. Cambridge, Massachusetts: MIT Press, 1995.

_____ . "Labor Market Effects of School Quality: Theory and Evidence." In *Does Money Matter?*, edited by Gary Burtless. 97-140. Washington, DC: Brookings Institution Press, 1996.

Chambers, Jay. *Report on $ and Personnel by Site in Ohio*. Washington, DC: National Center for Education Statistics, 1998.

Clune, W. H. "The Shift from Equity to Adequacy in School Finance." *Educational Policy* 8, 4 (1994): 376-95.

Cohen, M. C. "Issues in School-Level Analysis of Education Expenditure Data." *Journal of Education Finance* 22, 3 (1997): 255-79.

Cooper, Bruce. "School Site Cost Allocations: Testing a Microfinancial Model in 23 Districts in Ten States." Paper presented at the annual meeting of the American Education Finance Association, Albuquerque, New Mexico, March 1993.

Cooper, B. S. Personal communication, September 24, 1998.

Cooper, B. S.; R. Sarell; P. Darvas; F. Alfano; E. Meier; J. Samuels; and S. Heinbuch. "Making Money Matter in Education: A Micro-Financial Model for Determining School-Level Allocations, Efficiency, and Productivity." *Journal of Education Finance* 20, 1 (1994): 66-87.

Cubberley, E. P. *Public Education in the United States.* New York: Houghton Mifflin Co., 1919.

Darling-Hammond, L. *Teaching for High Standards: What Policymakers Need to Know and Be Able To Do.* Philadelphia: National Commission on Teaching and America's Future and the Consortium for Policy Research in Education, 1998.

Edison Project. *Annual Report on School Performance.* New York: Author, 1998.

Education Commission of the States. *Class Size Reduction Measures.* Author: Information Clearinghouse, 1998.

Farland, G. "Collection of Fiscal and Staffing Data at the School Site Level." *Journal of Education Finance* 22, 3 (1997): 280-90.

Ferguson, R. F. "Paying for Public Education: New Evidence on How and Why Money Matters." *Harvard Journal on Legislation* 28 (Summer 1991): 465-97.

Ferguson, R. F., and H. Ladd. "How and Why Money Matters: An Analysis of Alabama Schools." In *Holding Schools Accountable,* edited by H. Ladd. 265-98. Washington, DC: Brookings, 1996.

Firestone, W. A.; M. E. Goertz; B. Nagle; and M. F. Smelkinson. "Where Did the $800 Million Go? The First Years of New Jersey's Quality Education Act." *Educational Evaluation and Policy Analysis* 16, 4 (1994): 359-74.

Fox, James. "An Analysis of Classroom Spending." *Planning and Changing* 18, 3 (1987): 154-62.

Glass, G. V.; B. McGaw; and M. L. Smith. *Meta-Analysis in Social Research.* Beverly Hills, California: Sage, 1981.

Glass, G. V., and M. L. Smith. "Meta-Analysis of Research on Class Size and Achievement." *Educational Evaluation and Policy Analysis* 1, 1 (1979): 2-16.

Goertz, M. E. "The Challenges of Collecting School-Based Data." *Journal of Education Finance* 22, 3 (1997): 291-302.

Goertz, M. E., and L. Stiefel. "Introduction to the Special Issue." *Journal of Education Finance* 23, 4 (1998): 435-46.

Greene, Jay P.; William G. Howell; and Paul E. Peterson. "An Evaluation of the Cleveland Scholarship Program." Mimeo prepared for the Program on Policy and Governance, Harvard University, 1997.

Greene, Jay P.; Paul E. Peterson; and Jiangtao Du. "The Effectiveness of School Choice: The Milwaukee Experiment." (Occasional Paper 97-1). Cambridge, Massachusetts: Harvard University, Educational Policy and Governance, 1997.

Greenwald, R.; L. V. Hedges; and R. D. Laine. "The Effect of School Resources on Student Achievement." *Review of Educational Research* 66, 3 (1996a): 361-96.

_____ . "Interpreting Research on School Resources and Student Achievement: A Rejoinder to Hanushek." *Review of Educational Research* 66, 3 (1996b): 411-16.

Guthrie, J. W. "Reinventing Education Finance: Alternatives for Allocating Resources to Individual Schools." In *Selected Papers in School Finance, 1996,* edited by W. J. Fowler. 85-108. Washington, DC: U.S. Department of Education, Office of Educational Research and Improvement, 1998.

Guthrie, James W.; Michael W. Kirst; and Allan R. Odden. *Conditions of Education in California, 1989.* Berkeley, California: University of California, School of Education, Policy Analysis for California Education, 1990.

_____ . "Throwing Money at Schools." *Journal of Policy Analysis and Management* 1, 1 (1981): 19-41.

Hanushek, E. A. "The Economics of Schooling: Production and Efficiency in Public Schools." Journal of Economic Literature, 24, 3 (1986): 1141-77.

_____ . "The Impact of Differential Expenditures on School Performance." *Educational Researcher* 18, 4 (1989): 45-51.

_____ . "A More Complete Picture of School Resource Policies." *Review of Educational Research* 66, 3 (1996): 397-410.

_____ . "Assessing the Effects of School Resources on Student Performance: An Update." *Educational Evaluation and Policy Analysis* 19, 2 (1997): 141-64.

Hartman, William. "District Spending: What Do the Dollars Buy?" *Journal of Education Finance* 13, 4 (1988a): 436-59.

_____ . *School District Budgeting.* Englewood Cliffs, New Jersey: Prentice Hall, 1988b.

_____ . "District Spending Disparities Revisited." *Journal of Education Finance* 20, 1 (1994): 88-106.

Hayward, Gerald C. *The Two Million Dollar School.* Berkeley, California: University of California, School of Education, Policy Analysis for California Education, 1988.

Heckman, J.; A. Layne-Farrar; and P. Todd. "Does Measured School Quality Really Matter? An Examination of the Earnings-Quality Relationship." In *Does Money Matter?,* edited by Gary Burtless. 192-289. Washington, DC: Brookings Institution Press, 1996.

Hedges, L. V.; R. D. Laine; and R. Greenwald. "Does Money Matter? A Meta-Analysis of Studies of the Effects of Differential School Inputs on Student Outcomes." *Educational Researcher* 23, 3 (1994a): 5-14.

_____ . "Money Does Matter Somewhere: A Reply to Hanushek." *Educational Researcher* 23, 4 (1994b): 9-10.

Hentschke, Guilbert C. *School Business Administration: A Comparative Perspective.* Berkeley, California: McCutchan Publishing Company, 1986.

Herrington, C. D. "The Politics of School-Level Finance Data and State Policy Making." In *Where Does the Money Go? Resource Allocation in Elementary and Secondary Schools,* edited by Lawrence O. Picus and J. L. Wattenbarger. 1995 Yearbook of the American Education Finance Association. Newbury Park, California: Corwin Press, 1996.

Hertert, L. "Does Equal Funding for Districts Mean Equal Funding for Classroom Students? Evidence from California." In *Where Does the Money Go? Resource Allocation in Elementary and Secondary Schools,* edited by Lawrence O. Picus and J. L. Wattenbarger. 1995 Yearbook of the American Education Finance Association. Newbury Park, California: Corwin Press, 1996.

Isaacs, J. B.; M. S. Garet; and S. P. Broughman. "A Proposal for Collecting School-Level Resource Data on the Schools and Staffing Survey." In *Developments in School Finance,* edited by W. J. Fowler. 169-85. Washington, DC: U.S. Department of Education, Office of Educational Research and Improvement, 1998.

Johnson, G. E., and F. P. Stafford. "Social Returns to Quantity and Quality of Schooling." *Journal of Human Resources* 8 (Spring 1973): 139-55.

Kirst, Michael. "What Happens at the Local Level After School Finance Reform?" *Policy Analysis* 3, 1 (1977): 302-24.

Kruger, A. B. "Reassessing the View That American Schools Are Broken." *Federal Reserve Bank of New York Economic Policy Review* (March 1998): 29-43.

Laine, R. D.; R. Greenwald; and L. V. Hedges. "Money Does Matter: A Research Synthesis of a New Universe of Education Production Function Studies." In *Where Does the Money Go? Resource Allocation in Elementary and Secondary Schools,* edited by Lawrence O. Picus and J. L. Wattenbarger. 44-70. 1995 Yearbook of the American Education Finance Association. Newbury Park, California: Corwin Press, 1996.

Lankford, Hamilton, and James H. Wyckoff. "Where Has the Money Gone? An Analysis of School Spending in New York." *Educational Evaluation and Policy Analysis* 17, 2 (1995): 195-218.

Lawler, E. *High Involvement Management.* San Francisco: Jossey-Bass, 1986.

Marsh, D., and J. Sevilla. "Assessing the Costs of California's Middle School Reform." In *Restructuring School Finance for the 1990s,* edited by Allan Odden. New York: Jossey Bass, Inc, 1992.

Miles, K. H. "Freeing Resources for Improving Schools: A Case Study of Teacher Allocation in Boston Public Schools." *Educational Evaluation and Policy Analysis* 17, 4 (1995): 476-93.

Monk, D. H. "Challenges Surrounding the Collection and Use of Data for the Study of Finance and Productivity." *Journal of Education Finance* 22, 3 (1997): 303-16.

_____ . *Educational Finance: An Economic Approach.* New York: McGraw-Hill, 1990.

Monk, D. H.; C. E. Roellke; and B. O. Brent. *What Education Dollars Buy: An Examination of Resource Allocation Patterns in New York State Public School Systems.* Madison, Wisconsin: University of Wisconsin, Wisconsin Center for Education Research, Consortium for Policy Research in Education, 1996.

Monk, D. H., and S. Hussain. "Structural Influences on the Internal Allocation of School District Resources: Evidence from New York State." *Educational Evaluation and Policy Analysis* 22, 1 (2000): 1-26.

Monk, David H. "Educational Productivity Research: An Update and Assessment of Its Role in Education Finance Reform." *Educational Evaluation and Policy Analysis,* 14, 4 (1992): 307-32.

Mosteller, F. "The Tennessee Study of Class Size in the Early School Grades." *The Future of Children: Critical Issues for Children and Youths* 5 (Summer/Fall 1995): 113-27.

Nakib, Y. A. "Beyond District-Level Expenditures: Schooling Resource Allocation and Use in Florida." In *Where Does the Money Go? Resource Allocation in Elementary and Secondary Schools,* edited by Lawrence O. Picus and J. L. Wattenbarger. 1995 Yearbook of the American Education Finance Association. Newbury Park, California: Corwin Press, 1996.

National Center for Educational Statistics. *Digest of Educational Statistics, 1989.* Washington, D.C.: Author, 1989.

_____ . *Digest of Education Statistics, 1993.* Washington, DC: Author, 1993.

_____ . *Digest of Education Statistics, 1996.* Washington, DC: Author, 1996.

_____ . *Digest of Education Statistics, 1997.* Washington, DC: Author, 1997 http://nces.ed.gov/pubs/digest97

_____ . *Digest of Education Statistics, 1998.* Washington, DC: Author, 1998.

_____ . *Digest of Education Statistics, 1999.* Washington, DC: Author, 1999.

National Commission on Excellence and Equality in Education. *A Nation At Risk: The Imperative of Educational Reform.* Washington, DC: Author, 1983.

National Commission on Teaching and America's Future. *What Matters Most: Teaching in America.* New York: Teachers College Press, 1996.

National Commission on Time and Learning. *Prisoners of Time.* Washington, DC: U.S. Government Printing Office, 1994.

New American Schools. *Working Towards Excellence: Early Indicators from Schools Implementing New American Schools Designs.* Arlington, Virginia: Author, 1996.

Odden, A. "Class Size and Student Achievement: Research-Based Policy Alternatives." *Educational Evaluation and Policy Analysis* 12, 2 (1990): 213-27.

_____ . "The Finance Side of Implementing New American Schools." Paper prepared for the New American Schools, Alexandria, Virginia, 1997.

Odden, Allan, ed. *Education Policy Implementation.* Albany, New York: State University of New York Press, 1991.

Odden, A., and S. Archibald. "Reallocating Resources to Support Higher Student Achievement: An Empirical Look at Five Sites." *Journal of Education Finance* 25, 4 (2000): 545-64.

Odden, A., and C. Busch. *Financing Schools for High Performance.* San Francisco: Jossey-Bass, 1998.

Odden, A., and W. Massey. *Education Funding for Schools and Universities: Improving Productivity and Equity.* Madison: University of Wisconsin, Wisconsin Center for Education Research, Consortium for Policy Research in Education, Finance Center, 1993.

Odden, A.; D. Monk; Y. Nakib; and L. Picus. "The Story of the Education Dollar: No Academy Awards and No Fiscal Smoking Guns." *Phi Delta Kappan* 77, 2 (1995): 161-68.

Odden, Allan; Robert Palaich; and John Augenblick. *Analysis of the New York State School Finance System, 1977-78.* Denver, Colorado: Education Commission of the States, 1979.

Odden, A. R., and L. O. Picus. *School Finance: A Policy Perspective.* New York: McGraw Hill, 1992.

Odden, A. R., and L. O. Picus. *School Finance: A Policy Perspective.* 2nd Edition. New York: McGraw Hill, 2000.

Picus, Lawrence O. *The Allocation and Use of Educational Resources: School Level Evidence from the Schools and Staffing Survey.* Los Angeles: Center for Research in Education Finance, University of Southern California, 1993a.

_____ . *The Allocation and Use of Educational Resources: District Level Evidence from the Schools and Staffing Survey.* Los Angeles: Center for Research in Education Finance, University of Southern California, 1993b.

_____ . *The Effect of State Grant-In-Aid Policies on Local Government Decision Making: The Case of California School Finance.* Santa Monica, California: The RAND Corporation, 1988.

_____ . "The Local Impact of School Finance Reform in Four Texas School Districts." *Educational Evaluation and Policy Analysis* 16, 4 (1994a): 391-404.

_____ . "Estimating the Determinants of Pupil/Teacher Ratios: Evidence from the Schools and Staffing Survey." *Educational Considerations* 21, 2 (1994b): 44-52.

_____ . "The Local Impact of School Finance Reform in Texas." *Educational Evaluation and Policy Analysis* 16, 4 (1994c): 391-404.

_____ . (1994d). "Achieving Program Equity: Are Markets the Answer?" *Educational Policy* 8, 4 (1994d): 568-81.

_____ . "Using School-Level Finance Data: Endless Opportunity or Bottomless Pit?" *Journal of Education Finance* 22, 3 (1997a): 317-32.

_____ . "Does Money Matter in Education? A Policymaker's Guide." In *Selected Papers in School Finance 1995*, edited by W. J. Fowler. Washington DC: National Center for Education Statistics, 1997b.

_____ . "Defining Adequacy: Implications for School Business Officials." *School Business Affairs* 65, 1 (1999): 27-31.

Picus, Lawrence O., and Minaz Bhimani. "Estimating the Impact of District Characteristics on Pupil/Teacher Ratios." *Journal of the American Statistical Association*. Proceedings of the annual conference of the American Statistical Association, San Francisco, August 1993.

Picus, Lawrence O., and Minaz B. Fazal. "Why Do We Need To Know What Money Buys? Research on Resource Allocation Patterns in Elementary and Secondary Schools." In *Where Does the Money Go? Resource Allocation in Elementary and Secondary Schools*, edited by Lawrence O. Picus and J. L. Wattenbarger. 1995 Yearbook of the American Education Finance Association. Newbury Park, California: Corwin Press, 1996.

Picus, L. O.; D. T. Tetreault; and J. Murphy. *What Money Buys: Understanding the Allocation and Use of Educational Resources in California.* Madison, Wisconsin: Consortium for Policy Research in Education, The Finance Center, 1996.

Randall, E. V.; B. S. Cooper; S. T. Speakman; and D. Rosenfield. "The New Politics of Information in Education: Five Dimensions of the Change from District-Level to School Site Financial Analysis." In *Resource Allocation and Productivity in Education: Theory and Practice,* edited by W. T. Hartman and W. L. Boyd. 57-82. Westport, Connecticut: Greenwood Press, 1998.

Rothstein, R., and K. Miles. *Where Does the Money Go?* Washington, DC: Economic Policy Institute, 1995.

Rouse, Cecilia Elena, and Michele McLaughlin. "Can the Invisible Hand Improve Education? A Review of Competition and School Efficiency." Paper prepared for the National Research Council, National Academy of Sciences, Commission on Behavioral and Social Sciences and Education, 1999.

Sherman, J.; C. Best; and L. Luskin. *Assessment and Analysis of School-Level Expenditures.* Washington, DC: U.S. Department of Education, Office of Educational Research and Improvement, 1996.

Slavin, R. "Meta-Analysis in Education: How Has It Been Used?" *Educational Researcher* 13, 8 (1984): 24-27.

———. "Achievement Effects of Substantial Reductions in Class Size." In *School and Classroom Organization*, edited by R. Slavin. 247-57. Hillsdale, New Jersey: Erlbaum, 1989.

Speakman, S. T.; B. S. Cooper; H. Holsomback; J. May; and R. Sampieri. "The 3-Rs of Education Finance Reform: Re-Thinking, RE-Tooling and Re-Evaluating School Site Analysis." *Journal of Education Finance* 22, 4 (1997): 337-67.

Stringfield, S.; S. Ross; and L. Smith. *Bold Plans for School Restructuring: The New American Schools Designs.* Hillsdale, New Jersey: Erlbaum, 1996.

Sweetland, S. "Human Capital Theory: Foundations of a Field of Inquiry." *Review of Educational Research* 66, 3 (1996): 341-59.

Tetreault, D. Personal communication, October 7, 1998a.

Wenglinsky, H. *When Money Matters.* Princeton, New Jersey: Education Testing Service, 1997.

Wildavsky, A. *The New Politics of the Budgetary Process.* Glenview, Illinois: Scott, Foresman and Co., 1988.

Witte, John F. "The Milwaukee Voucher Experiment." *Educational Evaluation and Policy Analysis* 20, 4 (Winter 1998): 229-51.

Witte, John F.; Troy D. Sterr; and Christopher A. Thorn. "Fifth-Year Report: Milwaukee Parental Choice Program." Paper available from the University of Wisconsin-Madison, 1995.

Publications

Available from the ERIC Clearinghouse
on Educational Management

 In Search of More Productive Schools: A Guide to Resource Allocation in Education
Lawrence O. Picus • 2001 • 6x9 inches • xiii + 122 pages • perfect bind • ISBN 0-86552-147-6 • $12.75. CODE: EMOSMP

 Safe School Design: A Handbook for Educational Leaders *Applying the Principles of Crime Prevention Through Environmental Design*
Tod Schneider, Hill Walker, Jeffrey Sprague • 2000 • 8 ¹/₂ x 11 inches • xvi + 96 pages • perfect bind • ISBN 0-86552-148-4 • $18.00. CODE: EMOSSD

 Learning Experiences in School Renewal: An Exploration of Five Successful Programs
Bruce Joyce and Emily Calhoun • 1996 • 6 x 9 inches • viii + 208 pages • perfect bind • ISBN: 0-86552-133-6 • $14.50. Code: EMOLES

 Measuring Leadership: A Guide to Assessment for Development of School Executives
Larry Lashway • 1999 • 6x9 inches • viii + 117 pages • perfect bind • ISBN 0-86552-140-9 •$9.75. CODE: EMOMLG.

Roadmap to Restructuring: Charting the Course of Change in American Education
David T. Conley • Second Edition • 1997 • 6 x 9 inches • xvi + 571 pages • Cloth ISBN: 0-86552-136-0 ($34.95) Code: EMORMC • Paper ISBN 0-86552-137-9 ($23.95) CODE: EMORMP

 Leading with Vision
Larry Lashway • 1997 • 6 x 9 inches • xii + 148 pages • perfect bind • ISBN: 0-86552-138-7 • $13.50. CODE: EMOLWV

 School Leadership: Handbook for Excellence
Edited by Stuart C. Smith and Philip K. Piele • Third Edition • 1997 • xvi + 432 pages • Cloth ISBN 0-86552-134-4 ($29.95) Code: EMOSLC • Paper ISBN 0-86552-135-2 ($19.95) CODE: EMOSLP

 Student Motivation: Cultivating a Love of Learning
Linda Lumsden • 1999 • 6x9 inches • vi + 113 pages • perfect bind • ISBN 0-86552-141-7 •$9.50. CODE: EMOSMC.

How to Order: You may place an order by sending a check or money order, mailing or faxing a purchase order, or calling with a Visa or MasterCard number. Add 10% for S&H (minimum $4.00). Make payment to University of Oregon/ERIC. Shipping is by UPS ground or equivalent.

Telephone (800) 438-8841 • Fax (541) 346-2334

Publications Sales
ERIC Clearinghouse on Educational Management
5207 University of Oregon
Eugene, OR 97403-5207

You can also order online (with Visa or MasterCard) from our website—your gateway to information about educational policy and management.

http://eric.uoregon.edu